Reparations for Slavery

Lucent Library of Black History

Cherese Cartlidge

LUCENT BOOKS

An imprint of Thomson Gale, a part of The Thomson Corporation

THOMSON
™
GALE

Detroit • ondon

LIBRARY OF CONGRESS CATALOGING-IN-PUBLICATION DATA

Cartlidge, Cherese.
  Reparations for slavery / by Cherese Cartlidge.
    p. cm. — (Lucent library of Black history)
  Includes bibliographical references and index.
  ISBN-13: 978-1-59018-868-2 (hardcover)
  1. African Americans—Reparations—Juvenile literature. 2. Slavery—United States—History—Juvenile literature. 3. African Americans—Social conditions—Juvenile literature. I. Title.
  E185.89.R45C37 2007
  305.896'073—dc22
                                                                    2007024045

ISBN-10: 1-59018-868-3
Printed in the United States of America

Contents

Foreword

It has been more than 500 years since Africans were first brought to the New World in shackles, and over 140 years since slavery was formally abolished in the United States. Over 50 years have passed since the fallacy of "separate but equal" was obliterated in the American courts, and some forty years since the watershed Civil Rights Act of 1965 guaranteed the rights and liberties of all Americans, especially those of color. Over time, these changes have become celebrated landmarks in American history. In the twenty-first century, African American men and women are politicians, judges, diplomats, professors, deans, doctors, artists, athletes, business owners, and home owners. For many, the scars of the past have melted away in the opportunities that have been found in contemporary society. Observers such as Peter N. Kirsanow, who sits on the U.S. Commission of Civil Rights, point to these accomplishments and conclude, "The growing black middle class may be viewed as proof that most of the civil rights battles have been won."

In spite of these legal victories, however, prejudice and inequality have persisted in American society. In 2003, African Americans comprised just 12 percent of the nation's population, yet accounted for 44 percent of its prison inmates and 24 percent of its poor. Racially motivated hate crimes continue to appear on the pages of major newspapers in many American cities. Furthermore, many African Americans still experience either overt or muted racism in their daily lives. A 1996 study undertaken by Professor Nancy Krieger of the Harvard School of Public Health, for example, found that 80 percent of the African American participants reported having experienced racial discrimination in one or more settings, including at work or school, applying for housing and medical care, from the police or in the courts, and on the street or in a public setting.

It is for these reasons that many believe the struggle for racial equality and justice is far from over. These episodes of discrimination threaten to shatter the illusion that America has completely overcome its racist past, causing many black Americans to become increasingly frustrated and confused. Scholar and writer Ellis Cose has described this splintered state in the following way: "I have done everything I was supposed to do. I have stayed out of trouble with the law, gone to the right schools, and worked myself nearly to death. What more do they want? Why in God's name won't they accept me as a full human being?" For Cose and others, the struggle for equality and justice has yet to be fully achieved.

In many subtle yet important ways the traumatic experiences of slavery and segregation continue to inform the way race is discussed and experienced in the twenty-first century. Indeed, it is possible that America will always grapple with the fallout from its distressing past. Ulric Haynes, dean of the Hofstra University School of Business has said, "Perhaps race will always matter, given the historical circumstances under which we came to this country." But studying this past and understanding how it contributes to present-day dialogues about race and history in America is a critical component of contemporary education. To this end, the Lucent Library of Black History offers a thorough look at the experiences that have shaped the black community and the American people as a whole. Annotated bibliographies provide readers with ideas for further research, while fully documented primary and secondary source quotations enhance the text. Each book in the series explores a different episode of black history; together they provide students with a wealth of information as well as launching points for further study and discussion.

The Legacy of Slavery

From the earliest days of its history the United States has struggled with the issue of race relations. Slavery based on race was legal in this country for 250 years. From 1619, when the first Africans were brought to the settlement at Jamestown, Virginia, until the Civil War, white masters held blacks in a state of unpaid servitude. Blacks were seen as inferior to whites, with no legal rights whatsoever. It has been over 140 years since slavery was abolished and more than 40 years since segregation based on race was outlawed in the United States. Yet the long history of slavery and racial discrimination in the United States continues to affect the everyday lives of both blacks and whites today.

Many people think that racism is no longer a problem in the United States, that discrimination based on the color of a person's skin ended with the civil rights movement of the 1960s. Yet African Americans still face bigotry and discrimination. Halle Berry, for example, is one of the highest-paid actresses in the world and the first African American woman to receive the Academy Award in the Best Actress category. Yet despite her success, she says, she is not immune to racism in her daily life: "I don't care what anyone says—they may think it doesn't exist, but it's usually those who aren't black." She adds, "I've been called a nigger straight to my face."[1] Berry explains how racism affected her as a child: "I was black growing up in an all-white neighborhood, so I felt like I just didn't fit in. Like I wasn't as good as everybody else, or as smart."[2]

Like Berry, Molefi Kete Asante, a professor of African American studies at Temple University in Philadelphia, has witnessed racism firsthand. In his book *Erasing Racism* he writes about white racial privilege, racist attitudes toward blacks, the denial by whites that

Academy Award winner Halle Berry has experienced racism firsthand.

African Americans were injured by slavery and racism, and the feeling of many African Americans that they are strangers in their own country. Asante describes everyday racial discrimination experienced by African Americans in the United States:

> We walk into an automobile showroom and we are quoted higher prices than whites; we work as cooks in restaurants where whites with less skill and less time in the job are paid more; we step into employment agencies and they direct us away from jobs, high school guidance counselors direct us away from college, and college counselors direct us away from African American Studies courses where we can learn about our history and culture. We are told that there are no apartments available, but when our white friends call the same agency they are told there are several apartments available.[3]

Statistics show that conditions for African Americans today are indeed quite different from those for white Americans. Blacks fare much worse than whites when it comes to income, education, health, and criminal justice. According to data from the U.S. Census, the median income of blacks is only 64 percent that of whites; and 22 percent of blacks live in poverty, compared to only 9 percent of whites. While 30 percent of whites have college degrees, only 17 percent of blacks do. The infant mortality rate for blacks is more than twice that for whites, and blacks have a lower life expectancy rate than whites; a black person born in 1996 is expected to live 6.6 fewer years than a white person born in the same year. The fact that blacks make up only 13 percent of the U.S. population but account for 52 percent of the prison population points to a particularly glaring disparity between the races, as two African American scholars explain:

> Although no longer inscribed in law, this [racism] is implicit to processes of law enforcement, prosecution, and incarceration, guiding the behavior of police, prosecutors, judges, juries, wardens, and parole boards. Hence, African-Americans continue to experience higher rates of incarceration than do whites charged with similar crimes, endure longer sentences for the same classes of crimes perpetrated by whites, and, compared to white inmates, receive far less consideration by parole boards when being considered for release.[4]

Blacks account for half the prison population in the United States even though they make up only 13 percent of the general population.

John David Smith is a history professor who has written extensively about slavery, the Civil War, and racial discrimination. He describes the prevalence of racism in our country today: "Racism continues to stain the fabric of American society, north and south. Subtle, and not so subtle, acts of segregation, racial injustice, and racial violence are common in education, housing, government, law, business, and the arts. Racism and intolerance lurk in the corners of American culture like an incurable social cancer."[5] Yet many people today—including prominent citizens —discount the continuing effects of slavery and its legacy of legalized racial discrimination and segregation. For example, Frank Hargrove, a member of the Virginia House of Delegates, said of slavery, "I personally think that our black citizens should get over it." Hargrove added, "By golly, we're living in 2007."[6]

Hargrove's statement angered many people, because it is not so simple just to "get over" the effects of slavery. One expert on international human rights laws described slavery as a "terrible act of human oppression that has dominated our country for most of its existence."[7] On a trip to Africa, President George W. Bush declared: "The racial bigotry fed by slavery did not end with slavery or with segregation, and many of the issues that still trouble America have roots in that bitter experience of other times."[8] Roy L. Brooks, a law professor who has written extensively on race relations, perhaps summed it up best when he said, "The legacy of the past impinges on the present."[9]

It is no wonder then that many people—black as well as white—have joined the movement to obtain reparations for slavery in the United States. African Americans endured three centuries of slavery and another century of legalized racial discrimination, and the effects of generation after generation of

Invisible Man

In his award-winning semiautobiographical novel *Invisible Man*, written in the mid-twentieth century, Ralph Ellison depicted racial problems in the United States and explored the feeling many blacks have of being ignored. In the prologue to the novel, he described a phenomenon that many African Americans still experience today when he wrote:

> I am an invisible man. No, I am not a spook like those
> who haunted Edgar Allan Poe; nor am I one of your
> Hollywood-movie ectoplasms. I am a man of sub-
> stance, of flesh and bone, fiber and liquids—and I
> might even be said to possess a mind. I am invisible
> understand, simply because people refuse to see me. . . .
> When they approach me they see only my surround-
> ings, themselves, or figments of their imagination—
> indeed, everything and anything except me.

Ralph Ellison, *Invisible Man*. New York: Random House, 1980, p. 3.

Virginia politician Frank Hargrove angered many people with his statement that African Americans should "get over" slavery.

black citizens being denied equal opportunity are still apparent in American society today. Yet even though many people believe some form of compensation to African Americans is both deserved and necessary, reparations for slavery remains a highly controversial idea, and most efforts to obtain reparations for former slaves and their descendants have been unsuccessful.

Chapter One

What Are Reparations for Slavery?

When one person harms another, an apology or amends are frequently expected. Likewise, when a nation does harm to another nation or a group of people, some form of compensation for the wrongdoing is often sought by those injured. The movement to seek reparations, or amends, for slavery in the United States has become prominent in recent decades. Under slavery, millions of Africans were kidnapped from their families and homes and forced to work in a foreign land, where they had to give up their language and customs, were treated cruelly, and were not paid for their labor. Even after slavery was abolished in the 1860s, African Americans continued to be subjected to unfair treatment in the United States. Yet former slaves and their descendants have never received reparations for slavery, even though virtually everyone agrees that slavery was immoral and wrong.

What Are Reparations?

The word *reparations* shares the same Latin ancestor, and has a similar meaning, as the word *repair*. Both words have to do with restoring or fixing something that has been injured or damaged.

Reparations carries with it the idea of making amends for a wrong that has been committed. For example, nations that have been defeated in a war are often required to make reparations to other nations for the expenses incurred as a result of the conflict. Reparations are usually in the form of monetary payments but can include other things such as an admission of blame or wrongdoing, an apology, or restoring conquered lands to another nation. In the twentieth century the defeated nation of Germany was required to make reparations after both world wars to the victorious Allied

"A Healing of Our Psyches"

■

In his book *The Debt: What America Owes to Blacks*, Randall Robinson explains that demanding restitution for slavery would help African Americans gain a measure of self-awareness of their past as well as the damage done to them by the long history of enslavement:

> We would also show ourselves to be responding as any normal people would to victimization were we to assert collectively in our demands for restitution that, for 246 years and with the complicity of the United States government, hundreds of millions of black people endured unimaginable cruelties—kidnapping, sale as livestock, deaths in the millions during terror-filled sea voyages, backbreaking toil, beatings, rapes, castrations, maimings, murders. We would begin a healing of our psyches were the most public case made that whole peoples lost religions, languages, customs, histories, cultures, children, mothers, fathers. It would make us more forgiving of ourselves, more self-approving, more self-understanding to see, *really see*, that on three continents and a string of islands, survivors had little choice but to piece together whole new cultures from the rubble shards. . . . And they were never made whole. And never compensated. Not one red cent.

Randall Robinson, *The Debt: What America Owes to Blacks*. New York: Dutton, 2000, p. 208.

nations. Furthermore, Germany was required to accept sole responsibility for causing World War I.

But reparations are not made solely by nations defeated in war. Many groups of people around the world have received reparations for crimes committed against them, including Australian aborigines, New Zealand Maoris, and Jewish victims of the Holocaust. In the United States, Alaska natives and several Native American tribes have been paid millions of dollars in compensation for treaty violations and in some cases had their lands returned as well. Native Hawaiians received a formal apology from President Bill Clinton for the way in which the United States took over their nation in the late nineteenth century. And Japanese Americans who were held in internment camps during World War II also received an official apology and monetary reparations in the amount of twenty thousand dollars each from the U.S. government.

Japanese Americans arrive at an internment camp in 1942. The U.S. government later apologized for this act and granted monetary reparations to internees.

Many people think that the United States should make similar reparations for slavery to African Americans who are descended from former slaves. One organization that seeks such action is the National Coalition of Blacks for Reparations in America (N'COBRA). On its Web site, N'COBRA states:

> Reparations is a process of repairing, healing and restoring a people injured because of their group identity and in violation of their fundamental human rights by governments or corporations. Those groups that have been injured have the right to obtain from the government or corporation responsible for the injuries that which they need to repair and heal themselves. In addition to being a demand for justice, it is a principle of international human rights law.[10]

Because slavery in the United States ended so long ago, and because no former slaves are still alive, it is sometimes difficult for people to understand why anyone today would seek reparations for slavery. Raymond Winbush, a scholar and black activist, describes the reaction of many people to proposals for slave reparations: "Africans around the world have watched groups such as the Japanese, Jews, and others receive reparations for government-sanctioned crimes against them, while eyebrows are raised and arguments dismissed as nonsensical when similar justice for Africans and their descendants are made."[11] The current U.S. slave reparations movement stems not only from the conditions of American slavery but also from the continuing effects of centuries of racial discrimination that began with slavery.

The Racial Basis of Slavery

Slavery had existed throughout the world long before the American colonies were formed. But slavery as practiced in the Americas introduced a new element—that of race. Throughout history slaves had generally belonged to the same race as their masters. But in the colonies, "for the first time in history, dark skin became the social marker of chattel slavery,"[12] explains Brooks. This view of blacks as inferior to whites, which was used to justify enslaving Africans, continued to persist in American society long after slavery was abolished. Brooks explains the widespread and enduring effects of racially based slavery on African Americans:

For the first time in Western civilization, the slaves took serious note of the fact that master and slave were of different races. More than that, slavers targeted dark-skinned people and, not coincidentally, developed a racist ideology that sought to justify this practice—a social marker that affected free blacks as well and that continues to outlive slavery itself.[13]

In addition to being based on race, the institution of slavery in the American colonies and the newly formed United States was particularly harmful and brutal. Moreover, for the first time in history human beings were being transported in massive numbers thousands of miles across an ocean to be sold into bondage in an unfamiliar land.

The Transatlantic Slave Trade

In 1619 twenty African indentured servants became the first blacks to set foot in North America when they landed at Jamestown, Virginia. They were not slaves, however, because indentured servants could eventually gain their freedom. But by 1641 the Massachusetts Bay Colony had introduced slavery, making Africans permanent slaves. Other colonies soon did the same. It is impossible to know exactly the total number of people who were enslaved in the United States, because accurate records were not kept. But by 1781 there were approximately 575,000 men, women, and children held in slavery in the United States; by the outbreak of the Civil War 80 years later, that number had grown to 4 million.

In Africa people captured in war or kidnapped by neighboring tribes were marched in chains to the coast to be sold to European and American slave traders. Up to half of the captives did not survive the long march. Those who did faced a voyage across the Atlantic Ocean in severely overcrowded ships. Known as the Middle Passage, this voyage could take anywhere from three to ten weeks. Aboard the ships, humans were packed so tightly below deck at night that they could hardly move around at all. Some ship captains allowed the captives to come above the deck during the day, but others did not—meaning that some people spent the entire voyage confined to a cramped deck that was only 4 or 5 feet (1.2m to 1.5m) high.

An engraving depicts African slaves packed on the deck of a ship. Massive numbers of people were transported thousands of miles to be sold into bondage.

Life aboard the slave ships was miserable in the extreme. Not only were slaves regularly beaten and kept in chains, but exercise, food, and sanitary facilities were inadequate. Slaves were generally fed only two meals a day, which typically consisted of an unvarying diet of corn, rice, yams, or perhaps beans. Oftentimes the food and water became contaminated, but the slaves consumed it anyway because there was nothing else to eat or drink. Because of the unsanitary conditions created by so many people existing in such tight quarters, disease was rampant, especially dysentery. The men, women, and children aboard the slave ships also suffered from profound fear, anxiety, and depression; and some people, unable to handle the horrors, committed suicide by jumping overboard or simply refusing to eat.

Captured Africans are led to the coast to be sold to white slave traders.

It is estimated that 10 to 16 percent of the people shipped across the Atlantic perished aboard the slave ships. If they managed to survive the Middle Passage, slaves were then sold on the auction block like livestock. Even though the United States prohibited the further importation of slaves in 1808, slavery was still legal and continued to exist in the new nation, as generation after generation of African Americans were born into bondage.

The Brutal Institution of Slavery

Conditions for Africans enslaved in the United States were horrific. Slaves were seen by their masters as property, meaning they were considered less than human and had no legal rights. Their clothing, housing, diet, and medical care were inadequate, and they suffered from malnutrition and disease. Field slaves had to work long hours performing hard physical labor. Slaves who worked in their masters' houses were generally better treated, but all slaves were subject to harsh, cruel punishments, including whipping, maiming, and even castration. If a slave escaped, he or she was hunted down and severely punished if caught. A slave owner even had the legal right to put an uncooperative or rebellious slave to death.

The legal status of slaves and free blacks in the United States was officially defined by the Supreme Court when Dred Scott, a slave, sued for his freedom and that of his wife and children. In its 1857 decision in the case of *Dred Scott v. Sanford*, the Supreme Court declared that blacks were not U.S. citizens, and furthermore, defined them as "beings of an inferior order, and altogether unfit to associate with the white race, either in social or political relations; and so far inferior that they had no rights which the white man was bound to respect."[14] In fact, the U.S. Constitution counted each slave as only three-fifths of a person for purposes of determining population and political representation.

Slaves had no rights at all; even their marriages were not recognized as legal. Husbands could be sold away from wives, and children sold away from parents. There were even laws that made it illegal for a slave to learn to read or for anyone to attempt to educate a slave. An 1831 Mississippi law forbade any black, free or slave, to preach from the Bible; violators were to receive thirty-nine lashes with a whip.

Asante explains how the institution of slavery affected African Americans: "To deny freedom, will, culture, religion, and health is to create the most thorough conditions for loss. The Africans who were enslaved in America were among the most deprived humans in history."[15]

After Emancipation

After the Civil War the Thirteenth Amendment to the U.S. Constitution formally abolished slavery. For African

The slave Dred Scott filed a lawsuit in hopes of winning his freedom.

Americans who had been deprived of even the most basic rights, freedom represented challenges. Most had nothing when they were freed—no education, jobs, homes, or land. As one black man observed in August 1865, former slaves in Kansas and Missouri were "all most Thread less & Shoeless without food & no home to go [to] several of there Masters Run them off & as fur as I can see the hole Race will fall back if the U.S. Government dont pervid for them Some way or ruther."[16] Many former slaves were no better off than they had been during slavery.

Slavery was replaced by a system of sharecropping, in which former slaves continued to work on their master's lands for a share of the profits. White landowners often cheated the former slaves out of fair wages. A similar system was known as peonage, or convict labor—persons who were incarcerated could be leased out to work on farms or in chain gangs building roads. Under sharecropping and peonage, many freed slaves continued to live in conditions of extreme poverty and near-slavery, as Yuval Taylor explains in the book *I Was Born a Slave:*

> Although they were not called *slavery*, the . . . practices of peonage, forced convict labor, and to a lesser degree sharecropping essentially continued the institution of slavery well into the twentieth century, and were in some ways even worse. Peonage, for example, was a complex system in which a black man would be arrested for "vagrancy," another word for unemployment, ordered to pay a fine he could not afford, and incarcerated. A plantation owner would pay his fine and "hire" him until he could afford to pay off the fine himself: The peon was then forced to work, locked up at night, and, if he ran away, chased by bloodhounds until recaptured.[17]

In fact, there is evidence that although illegal, slavery actually continued in a modified form up until the 1950s. For example, in the 1920s and 1930s investigations by the National Association for the Advancement of Colored People (NAACP) found several instances of African Americans who were being forced to work on farms without pay. The landowners were prosecuted and sentenced to prison. And in 1954 two white men, the Dial brothers, were prosecuted for holding two black men in involuntary servitude on their farm in Sumpter County, Alabama. One of the men being held had attempted to escape from the farm but was captured and severely beaten. He died three days later. The Dial brothers received prison sentences in what writer Len Cooper referred to as "one of the last slavery convictions in the United States."[18]

Separate but Equal

The Civil War was followed by a period known as Reconstruction, which was the process of rebuilding the South and reuniting the nation. During Reconstruction, which lasted from 1865 to 1877, African Americans made several significant civil rights gains. The Fourteenth Amendment granted them citizenship rights and equal protection of the law, and the Fifteenth Amendment gave black males the right to vote. The Civil Rights Act of

Black convicts work on a chain gang.

1866 granted all citizens—black and white—equal rights to enter into contracts; sue; testify in court; and inherit, purchase, and sell property. During Reconstruction twenty-two African Americans were elected to Congress.

However, the successes of the Reconstruction period were short-lived, as many whites, particularly in the South, felt threatened by former slaves exercising their newfound freedoms. Reconstruction gave way to a period known as the Jim Crow era, which lasted until the 1960s. During this time southern states passed laws that restricted the equality and voting rights of blacks and prohibited blacks and whites from mingling in virtually every way. Blacks and whites had to use separate stores, post offices, public transportation, libraries, drinking fountains, hospitals, public parks, schools, and cemeteries. Marriages between the races were prohibited in all southern states. In 1896 the U.S. Supreme Court decided in the case of *Plessy v. Ferguson* that separating the two races was legal as long as public facilities, such as schools, were equal for blacks and whites. In truth, facilities for blacks were often poorly funded and inferior to those of whites, but this was hard to prove in court.

Young black students study in an all-black school during a time of segregation in the United States.

Jim Crow Destroys a Family

African Americans were terrorized by violence in the form of lynchings throughout the late nineteenth century and the twentieth century. But sometimes racial discrimination happened in more subtle, but equally harmful, ways. Writer Sarah Bracey White recalls growing up in the segregated South in the 1950s, when blacks were still paid less than whites for doing the exact same job. She describes the effect this had on her father and her entire family:

> Our long-absent father had once challenged the fairness of paying colored teachers less than white teachers, and joined the National Association for the Advancement of Colored People to seek equal pay. He was fired from his principal's job and blacklisted from teaching. Our family lost everything, and he started drinking heavily, then drifted away.

Quoted in Laurel Holliday, *Dreaming in Color, Living in Black and White: Our Own Stories of Growing Up Black in America.* New York: Archway, 2000, p. 43.

The racially repressive state laws of the Jim Crow era, as well as the Supreme Court decision in the *Plessy* case, meant that discrimination against African Americans in the United States was officially sanctioned by the government. Blacks were discriminated against in hiring practices, housing policies, and in the courts. One of the most heinous effects of slavery and the century of discrimination that followed was the violence perpetrated against blacks, often in the form of lynching—putting someone to death, usually in a brutal way, without benefit of a trial.

Lynching of blacks was common throughout the South after the Civil War and into the twentieth century. It was used as a means of controlling and terrorizing African Americans to prevent them from voting or holding public office and to deprive them of their rights. Usually the victims were accused, often falsely, of some crime against a white person—a crime that could be as minor as being disrespectful or whistling at a white woman. Lisa Delpit, an African American educator and author, explains the implications of this widespread violence against blacks: "If ever, heaven forbid, an actual or imagined crime was committed by a black person against a white person, then the well-being of all black people was at risk, often serious physical risk."[19]

The preferred method of lynching was to hang victims. The white perpetrators of lynching were seldom prosecuted, and in fact, many lynchings were attended by prominent citizens such as the mayor of a town. An estimated forty-seven hundred African Americans were lynched in the United States between 1882 and 1968, when such records ceased to be kept. But racially motivated violence against blacks continued to occur, and as recently as 1998 the brutal murder of an African American man named James Byrd, committed by three white men in Texas, was classified as a lynching because it was racially motivated.

The Civil Rights Era and Beyond

Segregation remained legal in the United States until 1954, when the Supreme Court overturned its earlier decision in *Plessy v. Ferguson*, declaring in the case of *Brown v. Board of Education* that separate schools for blacks and whites were unequal by their very nature and therefore unconstitutional. Throughout the rest of the 1950s and 1960s, as schools and other public facilities were ordered to desegregate, the civil rights movement tried to end Jim Crow practices and ensure that African Americans had equal rights.

But although African Americans today are legally protected from segregation and discrimination, the effects of their long deprivation in this country still remain. Asante, who calls for reparations in his book *Erasing Racism*, says: "The fact is, we cannot dispense with 250 years of involuntary servitude and sweep it under the rug. We cannot dispense with nearly one hundred years of official segregation."[20] Asante describes the continuing effects of slavery on life for African Americans in the United States today:

Justice, for the descendants of the millions of Africans enslaved during that terrible period of American history, has

The parents of James Byrd visit their son's grave. Byrd's murder in 1998 was classified as a lynching because the crime was racially motivated.

eluded our society, and discussion of it creates unusually harsh reactions from many Americans. The lingering effects of the enslavement are current and immediate in almost all sectors of American life: health, education, employment, housing, and law.[21]

Randall Robinson, a civil rights activist and the author of *The Debt: What America Owes to Blacks*, explains sentiments that are shared by many African Americans about their history:

No race, no ethnic or religious group, has suffered so much over so long a span as blacks have, and do still, at the hands of those who benefited, with the connivance of the United States government, from slavery and the century of legalized American racial hostility that followed it. It is a miracle that the victims—weary dark souls long shorn of a venerable and ancient identity—have survived at all, stymied as they are by the blocked roads to economic equality.[22]

"Only for White Kids"

■

Lisa Delpit, an African American educator and author, attended a segregated public school in Louisiana. Here, Delpit recalls watching the popular TV show *Romper Room* and describes how she became aware of racial discrimination as a child in the 1950s.

> I learned early that Miss Pat, of Romper Room—no matter how much I looked into her magic mirror and no matter how good a "Do-Bee" I was—would not let me join her television classroom. "That's only for white kids," my mother explained. Things weren't as they seemed on television. She had to explain the connectedness of things initially beyond the grasp of my four-year-old, home-centered mind: somehow my "nappy" hair and my family's brown skin (I had yet to understand that my own "lighter" skin was irrelevant as long as it was embedded within a brown family) was connected to the workings of the larger world in ways that prevented me from sitting in Miss Pat's circle or from going to the bathroom while shopping downtown—and prevented my mother from trying on hats in a department store or from getting a teaching job closer to our house.

Lisa Delpit, *Other People's Children: Cultural Conflict in the Classroom.* New York: New Press, 1995, p. 92.

Because reparations and apologies have been made to other groups of people and their descendants, it seems reasonable to many people that reparations should also be made to African American descendants of slaves. Brooks explains: "The government of the United States committed atrocities against black Americans for two and one-quarter centuries in the form of chattel slavery and for an additional one hundred years in the form of Jim Crow . . . and it has not even tendered an apology for either."[23]

Chapter Two

Early Efforts at Reparations

Initial efforts to obtain some form of compensation for slaves and their descendants began even before the end of the Civil War and continued for several decades. All of these efforts were unsuccessful, however. Well into the twentieth century, former slaves and their descendants continued to ask for reparations from the U.S. government, to no avail.

Forty Acres and a Mule: Sherman's Promise

The first attempt to provide some form of restitution to former slaves actually came a few months before the end of the Civil War, in January 1865. General William T. Sherman, whose famous march to the sea left a wide swath of the Confederacy in ruins, found his troops joined on the march by thousands of destitute and desperate newly freed slaves in need of food and shelter. Sherman issued Special Field Order No. 15, which outlined plans to distribute among former slaves lands that had been confiscated from slaveholders in South Carolina, Georgia, and Florida. The field order stated that each former slave family would get a 40-acre (16ha) plot of land and that "the islands from Charleston, south, the abandoned rice fields along the rivers for thirty miles back from the sea, and the country bordering the St. Johns River, Florida, are reserved and set apart for the settlement of the negroes now made free by the acts of war and the proclamation of the President of the United States."[24] Although mules were not specifically mentioned in Sherman's order, it was widely believed that they had been promised as well, and Sherman may have directed the army to distribute mules to the freedmen in order to till their lands. Thus, the phrase "forty acres and a mule" represented the promise made by the U.S. government to help the freed slaves start their new lives.

In March 1865 Congress established the Bureau of Refugees, Freedmen, and Abandoned Lands, commonly known as the

Freed black slaves spend time near their cabins on a South Carolina rice plantation in 1874.

Freedmen's Bureau, in part to help fulfill Sherman's order. The bureau was directed "to lease not more than forty acres of land within the Confederate states to each freedman or refugee for a period of three years; during or after the lease period, each occupant would be given the option to purchase the land for its value."[25] The bureau was in charge of a total of 800,000 acres (325,000ha) of land that had been abandoned by or confiscated from Confederate landowners. Within three months of the establishment of the Freedmen's Bureau, forty thousand former slaves had relocated and begun to farm 400,000 acres (162,000ha) of land they had been awarded in South Carolina and Georgia.

The Freedmen's Bureau

■

The Bureau of Refugees, Freedmen, and Abandoned Lands—more commonly known as the Freedmen's Bureau—is one example of government efforts during Reconstruction to help blacks overcome the disadvantages of enslavement. Established by Congress in March 1865, the bureau's main purpose was to provide food, medical supplies, and legal assistance to newly freed slaves after the Civil War. The Freedmen's Bureau also established schools to educate illiterate former slaves.

It was also in charge of distributing land that had been abandoned by or confiscated from southern landowners. These lands were supposed to be distributed in 40-acre (16ha) lots to former slaves and to those who proved they had been loyal to the Union during the war. However, most of this land was instead returned to its original owners. The Freedmen's Bureau was disbanded in 1869, although its educational efforts continued until 1872. Its most important accomplishment was in education for former slaves. It spent $5 million to establish free public schools and higher education for blacks in the South, including Howard, Fisk, and Atlanta universities and the Hampton Institute. By 1870 there were more than one thousand schools in the South for freedmen.

President Andrew Johnson pardoned Southern rebels and gave them land already promised to former slaves.

The land was, however, soon taken back from them. Not long after President Abraham Lincoln was assassinated, his successor, President Andrew Johnson, revoked the policies set forth by Sherman's order and the Freedmen's Bureau. Johnson granted a pardon to former rebels and returned their lands to them—lands that the former slaves had been promised and had begun to farm. According to Congressman John Conyers Jr., "Land that had been distributed to Freedmen was reclaimed by the federal government and routed to the enslavers (who had lost the Civil War, fought for the Confederacy, and had already benefited unjustly from the unpaid labor of Africans)."[26] Only about fifteen hundred of these former slaves were able to keep their land. Author and historian Mary Frances Berry describes the effect Johnson's actions had:

The government dashed the sea island freedmen's hopes after their hard work tilling land they thought was theirs. General Oliver Howard . . . was ordered to either persuade or force blacks occupying the land under Sherman's orders to abandon their claims to their former owners and return to work for them as laborers. Incredulous, the freedmen cried out at the betrayal.[27]

As a result of the government's broken promise, the phrase "forty acres and a mule" came to represent the failure of the U.S. government to provide compensation or adequate assistance to the newly freed slaves. The term is still used today in discussing the treatment of blacks in the United States since the end of slavery and the fact that reparations for slavery have not been made. Berry points out that "freedom for . . . ex-slaves would have been very different if the Union had kept its promises to give them land confiscated from Confederate slaveholders. The reparations question could have been settled at once."[28]

The Southern Homestead Act

A year after Sherman's unfulfilled promise, Congress enacted the Southern Homestead Act (1866). Under this act the head of a family received 80 acres (32ha) of land and was allowed six months to purchase the property at the low rate of only five dollars. This act applied to people of all races, not just former slaves, and was intended to encourage people to settle outside of heavily populated southern towns.

Approximately one thousand blacks received land under the act—far fewer than would have received land under Sherman's Special Field Order No. 15. The land distributed under this act was, however, generally of poor quality or was located in remote areas, and it was sometimes already claimed by lumber companies. In addition, most former slaves were desperately poor and therefore could not afford to purchase land, even at the special low rate. They also could not afford to feed and support themselves for months while they waited for their crops to come in. Scholars Ronald P. Salzberger and Mary C. Turck explain the outcome of the Southern Homestead Act for the freed slaves: "Whether by foreclosure or by terrorist threats, most black families lost the land they had purchased. Without land, they were once again reduced to dependence on white landowners and employers."[29]

The situation was not helped by Johnson, who vetoed any proposal to provide land to freed slaves. Among the proposals he refused to sign was one to colonize African Americans in the West, along the Union Pacific Railroad. There, they could have land as well as provide labor and protection to the railroad. Another proposal was to provide African American soldiers stationed in Texas with homesteads there and enough rations to survive until they could get crops going on their farms. Again, Johnson vetoed this plan. According to one researcher, "President Johnson seemed to be determined to make sure that freedmen received no land. He mercilessly vetoed any proposal having to do with providing land to the freedmen that reached his desk."[30]

Proposed Reparations Bills

In 1867 Congressman Thaddeus Stevens, who had been an outspoken opponent of slavery and was instrumental in getting the Fourteenth Amendment passed, introduced a bill in Congress, H.R. 20, called the African Slave Reparations Bill. It proposed to have public lands in all ten former Confederate states turned over to the

A family of black homesteaders, photographed in 1887, was one of the fortunate few that actually got land under the Southern Homestead Act.

federal government. Former slaves would receive 40 acres (16ha) of this land, along with fifty dollars per homestead. Under pressure from southern lawmakers, Johnson vetoed the bill. But the idea of seeking monetary compensation for former slaves did not die out.

The next attempt to aid former slaves was a bill seeking government pensions for African Americans. Black soldiers had fought in the Union army, and they and their families, including widows and children, were entitled to the same veterans' pensions provided to white veterans. But many blacks had trouble obtaining these pensions because they did not have the proper paperwork, such as birth certificates and marriage licenses.

The African Slave Reparations Bill

In 1867 Congressman Thaddeus Stevens, a longtime abolitionist, introduced the African Slave Reparations Bill in Congress. He spoke before the U.S. House of Representatives of the necessity of such a bill for former slaves and their descendants. The following is an excerpt from his speech:

> Four million persons have just been freed from a condition of dependence, wholly unacquainted with business transactions, kept systematically in ignorance of all their rights and of the common elements of education, without which none of any race are competent to earn an honest living. . . . Make them independent of their old masters, so that they may not be compelled to work for them upon unfair terms, which can only be done by giving them a small tract of land to cultivate for themselves. . . . Nothing is so likely to make a man a good citizen as to make him a freeholder. . . . Nothing will make men so industrious and moral as to let them feel that they are above want and are the owners of the soil which they till.

Quoted in Direct Black Action, "Thaddeus Stevens Speaks to Congress About Reparations for the African Slaves and Their Descendants." www.directblackaction.com/rep_bills/stevens_hr29.txt.

Under a proposed pension bill, former slaves over the age of seventy were to get a onetime payment and monthly stipend.

Partly for this reason, in 1890 Walter R. Vaughan, a white Democrat and a former editor of the Omaha, Nebraska, *Daily Democrat*, proposed a pension for former slaves that was modeled after the Union veterans' pension. He persuaded William J. Connell, his Nebraska congressman, to introduce the Ex-slave Pension and Bounty Bill in 1890. The bill considered any black person born before 1861 to have been a slave and therefore eligible for the proposed pension, unless other documentation was provided to prove they had not been enslaved. In addition, any caregivers for former slaves unable to care for themselves would be eligible for the pension.

The plan also called for onetime payments as well as monthly benefits that were based on the person's age and would increase in time. For example, former slaves who were over seventy years of age would receive a one-time payment (called a bounty) of five hundred dollars and a monthly pension of fifteen dollars. Former slaves who were between sixty and sixty-nine years of age would receive a bounty of three hundred dollars and a monthly pension of twelve dollars, which would increase to fifteen dollars a month when they reached age seventy.

Vaughan's interest in seeking pensions for former slaves was only partly motivated by a concern for the well-being of the freedmen and freedwomen in the South. Although he was disturbed at the state of poverty he witnessed among former slaves during a trip he took through Mississippi in 1870, he was also eager to help the economy of the South. Vaughan reasoned that if the former slaves received pensions, they would have more money to spend and thereby help revive the southern economy, which had been devastated by the Civil War. The bill was not, however, supported by the three black members of Congress, who instead advocated voting rights and federal aid for education as the way for blacks to escape from poverty. Ultimately, Congress rejected the pension bill, although other similar bills were proposed in the late 1890s.

In 1898 Congressman Jeremiah Botkin introduced a bill that would give former slaves 40-acre (16ha) homesteads, or 160 (64.75ha) acres for a family. This bill, which harkened back to Sherman's original promise of forty acres and a mule, did not pass. A Senate bill to appropriate one hundred thousand dollars to create a home in Washington, D.C., for elderly former slaves was sponsored by Senator George Perkins in 1895. One congressman said of this bill, "There is no question that the aged and colored people who once were slaves are more subject to destitution and require charitable aid more than any other class of people in the United States."[31] However, many black activists of the time were opposed to this bill, because the size of the proposed facility would have been much too small to accommodate all the former slaves who were in need. They also thought that if this bill passed, it would end the question of any other form of reparations.

Vaughan himself abandoned the pursuit of pensions for former slaves when the U.S. Post Office and the Pension Bureau investigated him for fraud. But the bill he had helped introduce would have a far-reaching effect for former slaves.

The National Ex-Slave Mutual Relief, Bounty, and Pension Association

Vaughan wrote a pamphlet titled *Freedmen's Pension Bill: A Plea for American Freedmen* that sold ten thousand copies at a dollar apiece in 1891. Several subsequent editions were released. This pamphlet caught the attention of several former slaves who in 1896 founded their own organization, the National Ex-Slave Mutual Relief, Bounty, and Pension Association, in Nashville, Tennessee. Two years later, a laundress named Callie House, who was

---

A Letter from Callie House

■

The following letter was sent by Callie House to the membership of the National Ex-Slave Mutual Relief, Bounty, and Pension Association after she was elected assistant secretary in 1898. The letter appeals to all organizations seeking the enactment of the Ex-slave Pension and Bounty Bill, also known as the Mason Bill, to work together in seeking compensation for former slaves.

It is my firm belief that honest labor should be rewarded, regardless of the color of the man or woman who performs that labor. I am in favor of the principles embodied in the so-called Mason Bill because they are just, and should the Bill receive the consideration it richly merits, it will, in my opinion, be but a question of time when those of our race who have borne the burden and heat of the day, will receive some recompense for honest labor performed during the dark and bitter days of slavery.

Let us consolidate all ex-slave organizations and bring to bear upon the law makers of the country which we labored so long and well to develop, every degree of influence within our power.

Very truly,
Callie House

Quoted in Mary Frances Berry, *My Face Is Black Is True: Callie House and the Struggle for Ex-Slave Reparations.* New York: Knopf, 2005, p. 78.

born into slavery, was elected the assistant secretary of the association. House became the driving force behind the organization and was considered to be its leader.

The purpose of the Ex-Slave Association was twofold. The first was lobbying to pass the pension bill. House traveled extensively throughout the South collecting petitions that included former slaves' names, ages, and the names of former masters. Thousands of African Americans signed these petitions, urging Congress to compensate them for their forced labor during slavery. The second purpose of the association was providing mutual assistance to its members, each of whom paid monthly dues of ten cents. By the early twentieth century the association had about three hundred thousand members. House stated, "If the Government had the right to free us she had a right to make some provision for us and since she did not make it soon after Emancipation she ought

Abolitionist Frederick Douglass supported the reparations movement.

to make it now."[32] Famed abolitionist Frederick Douglass supported the reparations movement, saying in a letter to Vaughan: "The Egyptian bondsmen went out with the spoils of his master, and the Russian serf was provided with farming tools and three acres of land with which to begin life,—but the Negro has neither spoils, implements nor lands, and today, he is practically a slave on the very plantation where formerly he was driven to toil under the lash."[33]

In 1915 House hired a well-known African American lawyer named Cornelius Jones to represent the Ex-Slave Association in a class action lawsuit against the U.S. Department of the Treasury. Jones calculated the value of the former slaves' labor to be $68 million. The money, Jones and House figured, would come from the cotton tax—a federal tax on confiscated raw cotton, first enacted in 1862 to help pay war debts. The money was still in a fund in the U.S. treasury, and since the federal government had profited from the sale of cotton produced through unpaid slave labor, Jones argued in federal court that the money should be paid to the former slaves. But the court rejected their claim. Secretary of the Treasury William McAdoo stated that the tax had been unconstitutional in the first place, and furthermore, "the money collected as a Civil War revenue tax has been treated as part of the general receipts of the Government and applied to payment of government debts. . . . There is no fund of $68,000,000 or any other sum in the Treasury of the United States for ex-slaves, or those who worked in the cotton fields of the South."[34] Jones appealed the case to the Supreme Court, which upheld the earlier decision.

Legal Problems

In addition to losing the lawsuit against the treasury, House and Jones faced other legal problems in their efforts to seek pensions for former slaves. Alarmed by the rapidly swelling membership of the Ex-Slave Association, as well as by the lawsuit, the federal government targeted the leaders of the association in an effort to stop their activities. According to Berry: "The government charged Jones with fraud for mailing letters seeking support from African Americans who might benefit from the lawsuit. The government sought to punish Jones for having the temerity to bring the lawsuit and for his connection to the Ex-Slave Association."[35]

Although the government ultimately decided against prosecuting Jones for fraud, they did bring charges of fraud against House and other leaders of the pension movement in 1916. According to one writer, House was charged with "acting fraudulently by collecting money to fund a lobbying effort that instilled the false hope in the hearts of the ex-slaves that the government would give them a pension."[36] The government's position was that because no such legislation for former slave pensions was likely ever to be passed, House and the other leaders of the movement were exploiting and defrauding people by taking money from them. Furthermore, the government charged that House had used funds she had collected for her own personal expenses.

Although there was no proof that she had misused any association funds, House was convicted and imprisoned for a year in the Missouri state prison. Her conviction and imprisonment led to the demise of the Ex-Slave Association's efforts to seek pensions, although the association continued to provide mutual assistance to its members. House died in 1928, and with her passing the association itself disbanded. But interest in the movement she had helped to found continued.

Marcus Garvey and the UNIA

Some of the former agents of the National Ex-Slave Mutual Relief, Bounty, and Pension Association turned to a new leader—Marcus Garvey. Born in Jamaica, Garvey had traveled extensively in South America, Central America, and England before moving to the United States in 1916. He had founded the Universal Negro Improvement Association (UNIA) in 1914, and he established several branches in the United States, ultimately attracting 2 million members worldwide. His organization, which supported civil rights, self-help, and racial pride in addition to reparations, attracted many of the same former slaves and children of former slaves who had belonged to the Ex-Slave Association.

Garvey and the UNIA saw repatriation, or returning, to Africa as the solution to the question of reparations for slavery. This idea was not new—the American Colonization Society had helped send about twelve thousand freed American slaves to the African nation of Liberia in the early 1800s. Garvey founded the Black Star Steamship Line in 1919 to transport former slaves and their

Marcus Garvey promoted the "Back to Africa" movement.

descendants to Africa. He sought to establish a black-governed country in Africa and petitioned the League of Nations after World War I for the former German colonies there, but was unsuccessful.

In 1922 the U.S. government brought the same charges of mail fraud against Garvey that they had brought against House. Garvey was convicted and spent two years in prison; upon his release he was deported to Jamaica. Garvey's conviction, imprisonment, and deportation brought about the end of the Black Star Steamship Line and the UNIA. However, many former members of the UNIA became advocates in the struggle for reparations, and Garvey's work continued to influence black leaders in the twentieth century, including the Black Muslims and Malcolm X.

The Ex-Slave Pension Movement Dies Out

Despite the demise of the Ex-Slave Association and the UNIA in the late 1920s, some aging former slaves continued to ask the government about pensions. In 1928 the relatives of a former slave asked John Sargent, the U.S. attorney general, "Is there any money set aside for old ex-slaves by the U.S. Government?"[37] Similar queries were sent to Presidents Herbert Hoover and Franklin D. Roosevelt in the 1930s. One former slave asked Roosevelt what had happened to the idea of "giving us pensions in payment for our long days of servitude?"[38]

Back to Africa

Early efforts to compensate freed blacks for slavery included the movement to send them back to Africa. In 1822 eighty-six free blacks were transported from the United States to Liberia with the help of the American Colonization Society, and another nineteen thousand followed in the next forty years. After the Civil War there was renewed interest in resettling blacks in Africa. However, African Americans sensed that whites simply wanted to get rid of the newly freed blacks by deporting them. Furthermore, most African Americans regarded the United States as their home and wanted to stay. Richard H. Cain, an African American congressman from South Carolina during the 1870s, spoke against the idea of repatriation:

> You have brought us here, and here we are going to
> stay. We are not going one foot or one inch from this
> land. Our mothers and fathers and our grandfathers
> and great-grandfathers have died here. Here we have
> sweated. Here we have toiled. Here we have made this
> country great and rich by our labor and toil. It is mean
> in you now to want to drive us away, after having
> taken all of our toil for two hundred years.

Quoted in John David Smith, *Black Voices from Reconstruction, 1865–1877*. Gainesville: University of Florida Press, 1997, p. 146.

Audley Moore petitioned the United Nations to force the United States to pay reparations for slavery.

One former member of the UNIA who continued the call for slave reparations was Audley Moore. Born in 1898, Moore was the descendant of former slaves; her grandmother had been the daughter of a slave-holder. Moore had a lifelong commitment to the civil rights movement, and as far back as World War I she organized the first organization to provide medical and other care to African American soldiers who were denied care for racial reasons by the Red Cross. In 1955 Moore founded the Reparations Committee of Descendants of United States Slaves, and in 1962 the committee filed a reparations claim in California.

In addition, Moore petitioned the United Nations in 1962 to demand that the United States be required to pay reparations for slavery. The following year, on the one hundredth anniversary of the signing of the Emancipation Proclamation in 1863, she presented President John F. Kennedy with a petition containing over a million signatures, demanding reparations from the government. Although none of Moore's efforts was successful, she continued as an active spokesperson for the reparations movement until her death in 1997.

The initial efforts to provide help and care for former slaves, including Reconstruction's forty acres and a mule, the congressional bills, and the pension movements, all failed to gain satisfactory recompense for the effects of slavery. Though ultimately unsuccessful, the work of former slaves and slave descendants like House, Garvey, and Moore laid the groundwork for the civil rights activists of the mid-twentieth century.

Chapter Three

Reparations Today

By the 1960s the focus of the reparations movement had shifted away from the idea of pensions for former slaves themselves—few, if any, former slaves were still alive by that time—and began to encompass the idea of reparations for the descendants of former slaves. There was also a growing belief among many blacks that African Americans should be compensated for the effects of the century of institutionalized racial discrimination and segregation that followed the Civil War. Segregation was viewed as a legacy of slavery; in fact, in the early 1960s Atlanta mayor Ivan Allen called it "slavery's stepchild."[39]

Calls for reparations came from African American civil rights leaders such as Martin Luther King Jr., Jesse Jackson, Malcolm X, Louis Farrakhan, and James Forman. Many attempts to obtain some form of reparations have been made in recent decades, such as lawsuits, proposed legislation, and demands for monetary payments and apologies. There has been some progress, but by and large a wide-scale program of reparations for slavery has remained elusive.

Civil Rights Leaders Demand Reparations for Slavery

The 1960s was a time of great social upheaval in the United States, including the civil rights movement. Civil rights leaders worked hard to guarantee the basic rights of citizenship for African Americans. One important piece of legislation was the Civil Rights Act of 1964, which banned discrimination in employment and public accommodations. Schools and universities began to be desegregated, as were other public facilities such as libraries and courthouses, as well as privately owned establishments such as restaurants, hotels, and theaters.

Representatives of various churches and community organizations demonstrate in Connecticut in 2002.

By the middle of the decade calls for reparations for slavery had been incorporated into the civil rights movement. One example of a public appeal for reparations came from King in his 1964 book *Why We Can't Wait*. King wrote:

No amount of gold could provide an adequate compensation for the exploitation and humiliation of the Negro in America down through the centuries. . . . Yet a price can be placed on unpaid wages. The ancient common law has always provided a remedy for the appropriation of the labor of one human being by another. This law should be made to apply for American Negroes. The payment should be in the form of a massive

Reparations Sought for Race Riots

In the 1920s two devastating race riots took place in the United States. The first occurred in Tulsa, Oklahoma, in 1921. The riot was sparked by false accusations of a black man raping a white woman. As many as three hundred people were killed by a white mob, and much of the predominantly African American Greenwood district was demolished. In 2000 a report commissioned by the state of Oklahoma recommended that $12 million in reparations be paid to the families of the victims. However, the state refused to pay. The governor said, "A state law prohibits Oklahoma from making reparations for any past mass crime committed by its officials or on the state's behalf."

A race riot that occurred in Rosewood, Florida, in 1923 was also sparked by the false claim of a white woman that she was raped by a black man. A white mob completely demolished an all-black neighborhood, burning houses to the ground and killing six black residents. The community was never rebuilt, and the twenty-five to thirty families who lived there lost their homes to the violence. In 1994 Florida passed the Rosewood Compensation Act, which paid each of the nine survivors $150,000 and created a scholarship fund.

Quoted in Raymond A. Winbush, ed., *Should America Pay? Slavery and the Raging Debate on Reparations.* New York: HarperCollins, 2003, p. 369.

program by the government of special, compensatory measures which could be regarded as a settlement in accordance with the accepted practice of common law.[40]

Another prominent civil rights activist, Malcolm X, also supported reparations for slavery. In 1964, after traveling and speaking in Africa, Malcolm gave a speech in Paris in which he explained his belief that reparations for slavery continued to be a valid issue a full century after slavery became illegal in the United States:

> The only reason that the present generation of white Americans are in a position of economic strength . . . is because their fathers worked our fathers for over 400 years with no pay. . . . We were sold from plantation to plantation like you sell a horse, or a cow, or a chicken, or a bushel of wheat. . . . All that money . . . is what gives the present generation of American whites the ability to walk around the earth with their chest out . . . like they have some kind of economic ingenuity.[41]

Prominent civil rights activist Malcolm X supported reparations for slavery.

Affirmative Action

The Civil Rights Act of 1964 also set up the Equal Employment Opportunity Commission, leading the way to the U.S. policy of affirmative action. Affirmative action was a way of ensuring that all job applicants and employees would be treated fairly, regardless of their race, religion, gender, or national origin. Furthermore, with affirmative action, minorities such as women and blacks were to be given preferential treatment in hiring practices and university admissions in order to make up for past discrimination against them. In this way, affirmative action can be seen as a form of reparations for slavery and racial discrimination. Although the practice of giving blacks preferential treatment is viewed by some people as a form of reverse discrimination—in other words, discriminating against whites—others, such as King and Presidents John F. Kennedy and Lyndon B. Johnson, saw it as a necessary and proactive method to compensate for the effects of decades of discriminatory hiring practices.

Johnson is viewed by many blacks as a champion of civil rights. At his funeral in 1973, one black woman stood before his casket and told her daughter, "People don't know it, but he did more for us than anybody, any president, ever did."[42] Johnson firmly believed in the policy of affirmative action. During a June 4, 1965, commencement address he delivered at Howard University (a predominantly African American school in Washington, D.C.), Johnson spoke of the problems African Americans faced as a result of slavery and segregation and explained why he believed affirmative action was fair:

> You do not wipe away the scars of centuries by saying: Now you are free to go where you want, and do as you desire, and choose the leaders you please.

> You do not take a person who, for years, has been hobbled by chains and liberate him, bring him up to the starting line of a race and then say, "you are free to compete with all the others," and still justly believe that you have been completely fair. . . .

> Perhaps most important—its influence radiating to every part of life—is the breakdown of the Negro family structure.

University of Michigan students demonstrate in 1998 to show support for affirmative action, a policy that some say is a form of reparations.

For this, most of all, white America must accept responsibility. It flows from centuries of oppression and persecution of the Negro man. It flows from the long years of degradation and discrimination, which have attacked his dignity and assaulted his ability to produce for his family.[43]

Johnson took concrete action to ease the effects of slavery and discrimination, including his War on Poverty, Great Society, and affirmative action programs. These programs, however, were

A "Devastating Heritage"

███

In the June 4, 1965, commencement address at Howard University in Washington, D.C., President Lyndon Johnson spoke of the great disparities between blacks and whites in terms of employment, income, poverty, and infant mortality rates. He said there were two main causes for the differences: the first was poverty, and the second was "the devastating heritage of long years of slavery; and a century of oppression, hatred, and injustice." Johnson continued:

> For Negro poverty is not white poverty. Many of its causes and many of its cures are the same. But there are differences—deep, corrosive, obstinate differences —radiating painful roots into the community, and into the family, and the nature of the individual.

> These differences are not racial differences. They are solely and simply the consequence of ancient brutality, past injustice, and present prejudice. They are anguishing to observe. For the Negro they are a constant reminder of oppression. For the white they are a constant reminder of guilt. But they must be faced and they must be dealt with and they must be overcome, if we are ever to reach the time when the only difference between Negroes and whites is the color of their skin.

Quoted in Lyndon Baines Johnson Library and Museum, "President Lyndon B. Johnson's Commencement Address at Howard University: 'To Fulfill These Rights.'" www.lbjlib.utexas.edu/johnson/archives.hom/speeches.hom/650604.asp.

abandoned by later administrations. And beginning in the mid-1990s states such as California, Washington, Texas, Louisiana, Mississippi, and Florida banned affirmative action in college admissions. Thus, the earlier gains of affirmative action are beginning to be reversed, and the perception many people have of unaddressed wrongs continues.

James Forman and the "Black Manifesto"

During the period of rapid political and social change in the late 1960s, James Forman came to the forefront of the reparations movement—and in a very dramatic way. Forman was an African American civil rights leader and the former executive director of the Student Nonviolent Coordinating Committee, which was dedicated to ending segregation in the South. In 1969 Forman and his supporters marched into the all-white Riverside Church in New York City, interrupting Sunday service. Forman stood at the pulpit and read aloud his "Black Manifesto," which was an appeal for reparations. The introduction to the manifesto begins with the words: "Brothers and Sisters: We have come from all over the country, burning with anger and despair not only with the miserable economic plight of our people, but fully aware that the racism on which the Western World was built dominates our lives."[44] The manifesto continues:

> We the black people . . . are fully aware that we have been forced to come together because racist white America has exploited our resources, our minds, our bodies, our labor. For centuries we have been forced to live as colonized people inside the United States, victimized by the most vicious, racist system in the world. We have helped to build the most industrial country in the world.[45]

Whereas previous civil rights leaders such as Malcolm X and King had called for reparations in broad terms, Forman's appeal was very specific. In the "Black Manifesto," he demanded $500 million in reparations from churches and synagogues for segregating and for exploiting blacks. Forman said this amount came to fifteen dollars for each black person in the United States. The manifesto outlined in detail how the funds were to be used—for example, for banks, publishing and printing, TV networks, a research center to study

James Forman reads from the "Black Manifesto" in 1969.

the problems of black people, a training center for blacks to gain a variety of communication skills, a better welfare system, and a black university in the South. All of these things, according to Forman, were "due us as a people who have been exploited and degraded, brutalized, killed and persecuted."[46]

Many people thought Forman's demands were unrealistic and excessive. An editorial in the *New York Times* stated, "There is neither wealth nor wisdom enough in the world to compensate in money for all the wrongs in history."[47] Black civil rights activist Bayard Rustin also criticized the "Black Manifesto," saying: "The idea of reparations is a ridiculous idea. If my great-grandfather picked cotton for 50 years, then he may deserve some money, but he's dead and gone and nobody owes me anything."[48]

Yet despite these criticisms, others supported the idea of reparations for slavery. In response to the "Black Manifesto," the religious journal *Christian Century* wrote: "We do not believe the idea of reparations is ridiculous. This generation of blacks continues to pay the price of earlier generations' slavery and subjugation; this generation of whites continues to enjoy the profits of racial exploitation."[49]

The "Black Manifesto" sparked controversy. But the controversy soon faded away, and Forman's demands for monetary compensation were not met. It would be two decades before another official proposal surrounding the issue of reparations was made, this time not from the pulpit of a church but from the floor of Congress.

Bills in Favor of Reparations

In 1989 Representative John Conyers Jr. of Michigan proposed a bill titled H.R. 40, the Commission to Study Reparation Proposals for African Americans Act. The bill proposes a seven-member commission to study the issue of reparations for U.S. slavery.

Slavery Reparations Scam

During the 1990s and early 2000s many African Americans filed so-called black tax claims with the Internal Revenue Service (IRS). They did this by reporting it on their tax returns as a tax credit for slavery reparations. Many of the claims were in the amount of $43,209 each, which was the estimated current value of forty acres and a mule. Other claims ranged all the way up to $100,000. However, the claims were fraudulent, because there was no such tax credit available. In 2001 eighty thousand such claims were filed, many of them by dishonest accountants and tax preparers who charged several hundred dollars to file the claims.

Several of these claims were actually paid in error by the IRS. Calling it the biggest tax scam they had ever seen, the IRS brought lawsuits against people who had prepared returns claiming the black tax. Anyone who received a refund in error by claiming the black tax had to repay it, with interest. Those who had already spent the money had to work out a repayment schedule with the IRS. In addition, some people have been fined $500 for filing frivolous tax returns.

Conyers was inspired to introduce the bill by the Civil Liberties Act of 1988, with which Congress apologized to Japanese Americans who had been detained in internment camps during World War II and paid them damages of twenty thousand dollars each. Conyers named his bill H.R. 40 because the number 40 holds a special significance for African Americans, as he explains: "I chose the number of the bill, 40, as a symbol of the forty acres and a mule that the United States initially promised freed slaves. This unfulfilled promise and the serious devastation that slavery had on African-American lives has never been officially recognized by the United States Government."[50] H.R. 40 seeks a formal apology for slavery in addition to a commission to study the aftereffects of slavery on African Americans and determine whether compensation is due to the descendants of former slaves. The opening paragraph of the bill states its purpose:

> To acknowledge the fundamental injustice, cruelty, brutality, and inhumanity of slavery in the United States and the 13 American colonies between 1619 and 1865 and to establish a commission to examine the institution of slavery, subsequent de jure [according to law] and de facto [in reality] racial and economic discrimination against African Americans, and the impact of these forces on living African Americans, to make recommendations to the Congress on appropriate remedies, and for other purposes.[51]

The bill does not make a proposal for specific reparations but merely asks for a commission to study the issue and make a recommendation on the matter. Although Conyers first introduced the bill in Congress nearly twenty years ago and has reintroduced it every year since, the bill has yet to make it out of committee, where the House of Representatives could vote on whether or not to send it to the Senate for further review. But the bill is gaining support, and in 1997, Representative Tony Hall of Ohio introduced a similar piece of legislation, H.R. 96, calling on the U.S. government to issue a formal apology for slavery. The bill was not adopted, but in 2000 Hall introduced H.R. 356, the Apology for Slavery Resolution. Like H.R. 96 before it and H.R. 40, Hall's second piece of proposed legislation has not made it out of committee. Hall wrote of the necessity for an official apology for slavery from the U.S. government:

Unfortunately, America's history is littered with many examples of missed opportunities to address the "peculiar institution" of slavery. When our Founding Fathers declared that "all men are created equal," we could have truly included everyone. When we established the Constitution as the rule of law for our new country, we could have treated slaves as full and equal, instead of treating them as three-fifths of a person.

When the Supreme Court made its rulings, when our nation amended the Constitution, or when Congress wrote Civil Rights laws—at any of these moments in our history, we could have apologized for slavery. But we failed, and now we must go back and finish our history's chapter on slavery.[52]

Like Hall's previous bill and the one introduced by Conyers, H.R. 356 seeks an official government acknowledgement and an apology for slavery but does not call for specific monetary compensation—a fact that has been criticized by proponents of the reparations movement, who say that both bills are not worded strongly enough.

Numerous other proposals at the state and city levels have met with various levels of success, including a reparations bill very

John Conyers Jr. has reintroduced H.R. 40 every year since 1989.

similar to H.R. 40 introduced in Michigan by State Representative Ed Vaughn. Also in Michigan, State Representative Derrick Hale introduced a bill that would allow tax credits for African Americans. These two Michigan bills have met with general opposition. California passed a law in 2000 that requires insurance companies to disclose their records on African Americans who were held as slaves. Similarly, cities including Philadelphia, Chicago, and Richmond, Virginia, require companies doing business with the city to disclose their historical ties to slavery, while Detroit and New Orleans are considering similar bills. New York City has adopted a resolution to study reparations for slave descendants. And California enacted a law requiring the University of California to research the economic legacy of slavery.

Lawsuits for Reparations

In addition to supporting such legislation, the reparations movement has gone to court. The most prominent and successful court case was brought by Deadria Farmer-Paellmann, a legal activist and the great-great-granddaughter of a slave. She filed a class-action lawsuit on behalf of 35 million African Americans in federal court. The lawsuit targeted the profits gained through slave labor by three companies: FleetBoston Financial, the insurance company Aetna, and the railroad firm CSX. Farmer-Paellmann explains, "These are corporations that benefited from stealing people, from stealing labor, from forced breeding, from torture, from committing numerous horrendous acts, and there's no reason why they should be able to hold onto assets they acquired through such horrendous acts."[53]

FleetBoston is the successor to Providence Bank, which the lawsuit says was founded by John Brown, a Rhode Island slave trader. Likewise, CSX is the successor to various railroads that were built and run in part with slave labor, according to the lawsuit. And Aetna issued slave life insurance policies to slaveholders, thereby benefiting from the slave trade. According to Farmer-Paellmann:

> Slave life insurance policies were written with slave holders as the beneficiaries. An investor, unsure about purchasing costly human chattel, would gain security from predecessor companies to Aetna Inc., New York Life Insurance Company, even Ameri-

can International Group. The policies essentially meant: "go ahead and buy those Africans. If they die, we've got you covered. You can buy another one." Slave policies helped slave owners to employ enslaved Africans in ultra hazardous capacities. Consequently, insured enslaved Africans sometimes died horrendous deaths—for example, drowning or burning to death in coal mines.[54]

As a result of this lawsuit, Aetna apologized to African Americans in March 2000 for its role in supporting slavery. It also made reparations by establishing a scholarship fund and internship program for minorities. The suit brought by Farmer-Paellmann prompted the California law that requires all insurance companies operating in the state to research their records for slave life insurance policies.

In 2005 the NAACP announced that it would pursue reparations from private businesses that benefited from slavery. Members of the group also planned to boycott any company that refused to participate in the association's annual business diversity report card. "Absolutely, we will be pursuing reparations from companies that have historical ties to slavery and engaging all parties to come to the table," said Dennis C. Hayes, interim president and chief executive officer of the NAACP. Hayes added, "Many of the problems we have

Lawyer Deadria Farmer-Paellmann has filed lawsuits seeking reparations from private companies that she claims once benefited from slave labor.

now including poverty, disparities in health care and incarcerations can be directly tied to slavery."[55]

Apologies for Slavery

Apologizing to African Americans for slavery, as Aetna did, is viewed as a form of reparation. Public apologies, while mostly symbolic gestures, are seen as an important step toward reconciliation and healing past wounds. There have been several public

A sale bill poster from 1829 advertises a public auction of slaves in the West Indies.

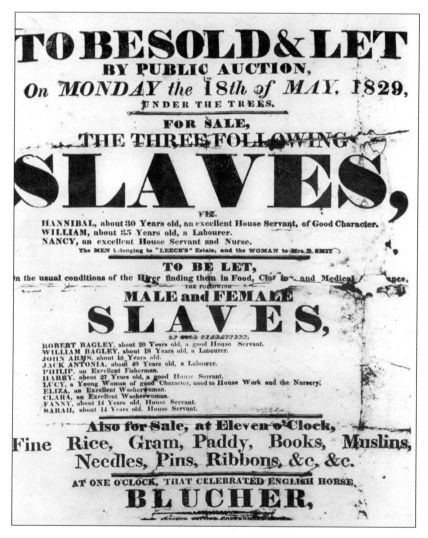

apologies in recent years, including one issued on the front page of the *Hartford Courant* in 2000. The Connecticut newspaper apologized for having run advertisements for slave auctions in the past. Other prominent groups and companies have apologized publicly for their role in slavery and racism, including the Southern Baptist Convention, JP Morgan Chase, and Wachovia.

In February 2007 Virginia became the first state to issue an official apology for its role in slavery. The state expressed "profound regret for the commonwealth's role in sanctioning the immoral institution of human slavery, in the historic wrongs visited upon native peoples, and in all other forms of discrimination and injustice that have been rooted in racial and cultural bias and misunderstanding."[56]

The fact that Virginia was the place where the first African Americans in the New World arrived makes the apology especially significant. According to the official resolution:

[Government-sanctioned slavery] ranks as the most horrendous of all depredations of human rights and violations of our founding ideals in our nation's history, and the abolition of slavery was followed by systematic discrimination, enforced segregation, and other insidious institutions and practices toward Americans of African descent that were rooted in racism, racial bias, and racial misunderstanding.[57]

In March 2007 Maryland followed the lead of Virginia and offered an official apology for slavery, expressing "profound regret for the role that Maryland played in instituting and maintaining slavery and for the discrimination that was slavery's legacy."[58] Other states, including Missouri, North Carolina, and Georgia, are considering issuing similar apologies. The U.S. government, however, has not officially apologized for its role in slavery. Presidents Clinton and George W. Bush, as well as Tony Blair, prime minister of the United Kingdom, have come close by saying that slavery was wrong but have stopped short of actual apologies.

Efforts to obtain reparations for slavery continue, however, and the reparations movement has been gaining supporters in recent years. While some successes in various forms have been achieved, no real reparations for slavery as such have been offered. One reason is that this is a very controversial issue. It is also an extremely complicated one, with many practical problems.

Chapter Four

The Complexities of Reparations

Any program of reparations to descendants of slaves would be difficult to define and carry out for a variety of reasons. One of the biggest problems involved in dealing with the issue of reparations is the fact that so much time has passed since slavery and segregation ended. There are also numerous questions that would need to be addressed, such as what form reparations should take and who should pay for them. All of these questions and concerns complicate the issue and make it a difficult one to resolve.

The Passage of Time

Slavery was officially abolished in the United States more than 140 years ago, and legalized segregation ended more than 40 years ago. The fact that so much time has passed since abolition and the civil rights movement complicates efforts to obtain reparations for slavery and its aftermath in several ways. First of all, with the passage of time, it becomes increasingly difficult to trace people's ancestry and therefore determine their level or degree of victimization or guilt. Second, the passage of so much time allows the introduction of new factors into the reparations equation, such as people who immigrated to the United States after slavery was abolished. Are recent white immigrants responsible for contributing to reparations? Are recent black immigrants entitled to receive reparations? And identifying descendants of slaves and slaveholders has been made more complicated by the racial mixing that has taken place during the passage of all this time—many biracial people are descendants of *both* slaves and of slaveholders.

There is also the question of the statute of limitations. Statutes of limitations are laws that regulate how long after a crime has been committed that legal action concerning the crime may begin. If a crime is not prosecuted within this length of time, then

Many biracial Americans are descendents of both slaves and slaveholders.

the victim or victims lose the right to seek legal redress for the crime. These limitations are in place because with the passage of time it becomes more difficult to prosecute a crime fairly, since evidence may be lost and people's memories of details surrounding the crime begin to fade. The length of statutes of limitations varies depending on the crime, with more serious crimes having a longer statute of limitations. Less serious crimes, known as misdemeanors, may have a statute of limitations of two years. Some crimes, such as murder, war crimes, and crimes against humanity, have no statute of limitations on them, meaning that charges can be brought no matter how long ago the crime occurred.

In the case of reparations for slavery, the question of a statute of limitations represents another problem because it is unclear what the time limit is or whether a limit exists at all. Moore brought her claim in California in 1962, ninety-seven years after the abolition of slavery, because she read "in an old Methodist encyclopedia that a captive people have one hundred years to state their judicial claims against their captors or international law will consider you satisfied with your condition."[59] But other people say there is no statute of limitations when it comes to slavery because it was a human rights abuse. As Robinson points out, "We are talking about crimes by governments against people, crimes that should not be touched by statutes of limitations, because when governments commit such crimes, they 'have a certain immortality.'"[60]

Law professor Jon M. van Dyke agrees that the statue of limitations should not apply to the enslavement of blacks in America because it constituted a crime against humanity. He also believes that slavery should be exempt from any statute of limitations because of what is known as equitable tolling, which suspends time limits in cases where the victim or victims are prevented from seeking legal action at an earlier date. Van Dyke states, "It certainly would have been unrealistic for African Americans to have brought a suit for reparations at any time prior to the present period, since they were subject to active, officially sanctioned discrimination until recently."[61] Furthermore, van Dyke asserts that "the duty to address violations of fundamental human rights continues as long as the consequences of those violations continue to scar a community."[62]

But if there is no statute of limitations on human rights crimes, then how far back in history are people allowed to go in seeking reparations for past wrongs? Some people wonder whether allowing African Americans to sue for reparations and apologies for slavery would open the doors to other groups suing for ancient offenses. For example, novelist and former U.S. poet laureate Robert Penn Warren asks, "Is the Greek government responsible for paying reparation to the descendants of Athenian helots [who were defeated in the Peloponnesian War in the fifth century B.C.]? Would the descendants of a mill girl in Lowell, Massachusetts, who died of lint-lungs in 1845, have a claim on Washington, D.C. in 1965?"[63] Similarly, Delegate Frank D. Hargrove of Virginia pointed out the problems of addressing past wrongs when he asked, "Are we going to force the Jews to apologize for killing Christ?"[64]

While Warren's and Hargrove's comments take things to an extreme, there are in fact precedents for making restitution and apologies today for acts that occurred as long ago as the mid-nineteenth century. For example, Blair apologized to the Irish for the way the British government treated their ancestors during a famine in Ireland that lasted from 1845 to 1850. In the United States the Sand Creek Massacre National Historic Study Site Act offered an official apology for an attack by U.S. soldiers on a Cheyenne village in Colorado, in which hundreds of women and children were killed. The attack occurred in 1864—before the end of the Civil War.

Who Should Pay Reparations for Slavery?

The issue of a statute of limitations aside, the fact remains that no former slaves or former slaveholders are still alive. This represents a problem. As Salzberger and Turck ask, "How are we to deal with old, even ancient injustices, when the current population contains neither the immediate victims nor the perpetrators?"[65] One answer to this question that may seem obvious is for the descendants of slaveholders to pay reparations to the descendants of slaves. But this idea is not as simple as it sounds. For one thing, the U.S. Census does not track descent from slaves or slave owners. It would be possible, of course, to use other sorts of historical records to track down who is descended from former

An illustration depicts the Sand Creek Massacre of 1864.

slaveholders and seek reparations from them, but even this approach has its problems. Again, because so much time has passed and today's population is several generations removed from slavery, it is likely that many white people are descended from both slaveholders and abolitionists—people who did not own slaves and fought to end slavery. Many people argue that descendants of white abolitionists and Union soldiers who fought to free the slaves should not be required to pay reparations.

Likewise, many people believe that recent immigrants, as well as descendants of immigrants who arrived in the United States after the Civil War, should not have to share the financial burden of paying reparations for something that happened before they or their ancestors arrived in this country. But van Dyke points out that "white people, speaking generally, continue to benefit from the burdens that were imposed for hundreds of years on Blacks. Even those whites whose ancestors immigrated to the United States after the

Civil War benefit from the white skin privilege that still brings substantial benefits in our country."[66] Brooks agrees, arguing that when someone immigrates to a country, he or she must accept the positive as well as the negative aspects of that country. This means that immigrants to the United States, for example, enjoy its freedoms but must also contribute to paying off a national debt that was incurred before they arrived. Brooks says: "Whether a recent arrival or a member of an old-line family, an inhabitant of a country cannot pick and choose from among aspects of the country's history. Certainly the nation's largest and longest moral debt, slavery carries over from generation to generation until it is paid off."[67]

Some people believe that even the descendants of whites who fought in the Civil War or took risks to speak out against segregation should contribute to paying reparations, since they are all part of the United States. Van Dyke states:

> Those whose ancestors participated in these noble initiatives, as well as those whose ancestors were not slave owners, may ask why they should now have to participate in reparations payments. They should not have to pay as individuals, of course, but it is still their country that authorized and sustained, through laws, courts, and police enforcement, an oppressive system that continues to stain our communities with discriminatory perceptions, beliefs, and practices. Because all white Americans benefit by being white, we all must participate in providing the economic compensation necessary to restore to the African Americans the property that was taken from them through the institution of slavery and its aftermath.[68]

Asante agrees that since all white people, regardless of whether their ancestors owned slaves or not, profit from being the privileged class in the United States, all whites are responsible for paying reparations. He also points out that, in addition to insurance companies, railroad firms, and financial institutions such as those sued by Deadria Farmer-Paellmann, American universities such as Harvard and Yale have ties to the slave trade, which illustrates how pervasive the benefits of slavery were for whites:

> Yale University students discovered in 2001 that their institution was founded with money made from the dirty business of the slave trade. But Yale is not alone; profiting from

the enslavement of Africans was a national project, not merely an individual corporate or personal one. There were individual whites who had nothing to do with the enslavement of blacks per se. Of course, most whites participated in the privilege that came with whiteness in a racist society, and there is culpability when one receives the rewards of someone else's suffering and degradation. The fact that one of the most prestigious universities in the nation has a history intertwined with the slave trade only demonstrates the extent of the crime.[69]

Yet, as Salzberger and Turck point out, "How, if at all, is responsibility for an injustice to be justly distributed among members of a group when some of those members were not themselves the causes of the deeds that cry out for remedy?"[70] Robert K. Fullinwider, a

Union soldiers enjoy a few moments of peace. Some people believe that descendants of those who fought in the Civil War should pay slavery reparations.

Other Models of Reparations

◾

Other examples of reparations paid by governments to groups of people for past wrongs might be used as models for a program of reparations for slavery. There are several examples around the world of reparations being made to a group of people. One that seems particularly relevant is the case of the Japanese Americans who were forced into internment camps during World War II. The Civil Liberties Act of 1988 offered an official apology and twenty thousand dollars in reparations to each survivor or his or her surviving spouse or children. Another related example is the reparations paid by Germany to survivors of the Jewish Holocaust in World War II. The biggest difference between these two cases and that of reparations for slavery is that no former slaves and extremely few of their children are still alive, whereas direct victims of the Holocaust and the Japanese American internment were still living. As David Horowitz says, in these and other cases, "the recipients of reparations were the direct victims of the injustice or their immediate families. This would be the only case of reparations to people who were not immediately affected and whose sole qualification to receive reparations would be racial."

David Horowitz, *Uncivil Wars: The Controversy over Reparations for Slavery.* San Francisco: Encounter, 2002, p. 13.

philosopher, makes the argument that if a nation owes a debt, then its citizens are required to pay their share of that debt. The reparations for Japanese Americans, for example, were paid out of American taxpayer dollars. Fullinwider says: "One can make a parallel argument for reparations to African Americans. . . . Just as it was the nation that owed Japanese Americans reparations, so it is the nation that owes reparations to African Americans. And so it is that Americans not as individuals but as citizens owe support for the nation's debt."[71]

One approach would be to follow the example of German companies that were involved in slave labor during World War II.

In 2001 these companies, as well as the German government, paid into a $5 billion fund established for the victims. The amounts paid by each company varied according to the scope of each corporation's business activities. Van Dyke suggests, "Utilizing this approach, the Southern states and the federal government, plus those companies that benefited or profited from slavery, should contribute to the reparations fund."[72] Further, Brooks argues that because white southerners actually fought to retain the institution of slavery, "white southerners carry additional responsibility"[73] when it comes to payment of reparations.

Who Should Get Reparations for Slavery?

Just as it is difficult to determine who should pay reparations for slavery, it is also difficult to determine who should receive reparations. The fact that the U.S. Census does not track descent from slaves is compounded by the fact that in many cases, accurate records on slaves were not kept. For example, many slaves did not have birth certificates, and since their marriages were not legally recognized they often lacked marriage certificates as well. Oftentimes families were separated by masters who sold slaves to another owner, making the descendants of slaves difficult to trace—more difficult than the descendants of slaveholders. In addition, not every African American in the United States today can be assumed to be descended from slaves, so race alone would not be enough to determine eligibility for reparations. The difficulties involved in identifying the victims of slavery and discrimination create problems when it comes to determining who should be eligible for reparations. Fullinwider asks: "Should every individual black person receive reparations? Quite obviously, different blacks have fared very differently under past segregation. Most of those affected worst are long dead."[74]

Even if it could be agreed that reparations were due to every black person because of the effects of racial discrimination, this still raises problems in identifying recipients. The fact that so many people are of mixed race makes it difficult to determine who should be entitled to reparations. Are people who classify themselves as white, but who may have a distant ancestor who was black, entitled to reparations? Likewise, because of the numerous instances of white slave owners impregnating their

An enslaved woman shows anguish at being taken from her child.

women slaves, as well as the increase in racially mixed marriages throughout the twentieth century, many people who classify themselves as black today may have several ancestors who were white. Boris Bittker explains the difficulty that could arise: "There has been enough mating across racial lines in the United States to justify the prediction that hundreds of thousands, if not millions, of persons of debatable racial composition might apply for compensation if the benefits were worth pursuing."[75]

Some Problems with Reparations

———————————◼———————————

Kimberley Jane Wilson is a conservative African American writer. Here she echoes the concerns shared by many people over the complexities of reparations for slavery:

> Will every black person who can prove he or she is a descendant of slaves get a check? Will we all get a tax credit? Will every black child get a scholarship to the college of their choice? How black do you have to be to get reparations? If one of your parents or grandparents is white, are you still eligible? . . .

> Will we be getting reparations from Great Britain? After all, colonial America belonged to England when slavery was introduced here in 1619. Do Native Americans owe us reparations? Some tribes took an active part in owning slaves. In fact, there were even free blacks who purchased slaves. Do the descendants of these people owe reparations? . . .

> No amount of apologies and no amount of cash can wash away the sin of slavery. Giving me a check as "compensation" for the agony of my ancestors trivializes their suffering. I feel uneasy at the thought of making a profit from that suffering.

Kimberley Jane Wilson, "Reparations, Anyone?" Project 21. www.nationalcenter.org/P21NVWil sonReparations801.html.

Most people would agree that to be entitled to reparations for racial discrimination and segregation, a person of mixed race must have suffered the effects of discrimination and segregation. But proving that would be extremely difficult. In addition, there is little consensus about whether a person who is half black should be entitled to half as much in reparations, and a person who is one-fourth black be entitled to one-fourth as much, and so on, or whether everyone should get the same amount. Similarly, Fullinwider asks, "Do we pay the same to the child of middle class blacks who immigrated to the United States from the West Indies twenty years ago that we pay to an elderly retiree who spent half his life as a field hand in Mississippi?"[76]

How Much Should Be Paid?

Estimates of what it would cost to pay reparations for slavery range into the billions and even trillions of dollars. Some examples of dollar amounts that have been called for include Forman's $500 million, while Bittker reports the estimated present-day value of unpaid slave labor would be between $448 and $995 billion, and Farmer-Paellmann puts that figure at $1.4 trillion. Columnist Jonah Goldberg points out that some people call for $100,000 for a family of four, while others call for $100,000 for each individual; he estimates that "for a country that has at minimum 36.4 million people who call themselves black or African-American,"[77] the total amount might come to something around $3 trillion. A professor at Georgetown named Richard America, who wrote *Paying the Debt: What White America Owes Black America*, estimates the U.S. government owes African Americans $5 trillion to $10 trillion. Jack White, a writer for *Time* magazine who is the grandson of a slave, figures the amount owed for the unpaid wages of 10 million slaves for nearly 250 years, plus compensation for pain and suffering, with interest, amounts to $24 trillion.

In answer to the question of how much is owed, the group N'COBRA explains:

> Once we know how much damage has been done to us, and what is required to repair the damage, we will know how much is owed. We cannot allow anyone to offer, or accept on our behalf, some arbitrary figure based on some other peoples' reparations settlement. For example, the four year internment of Japanese in America, or the five year holocaust of Jewish people in Europe may require a different set of remedies than the 500 years holocaust of Africans in America. The nature and extent of the damage and the number of people impacted will dictate the type, duration, and amount of reparations owed. Some estimate eight trillion dollars.[78]

What Form Should Reparations Take?

Another difficulty in determining a program of reparations is the question of whether they should be made in the form of individual payments, as was done with the Japanese Americans, or in the form of increased funding for health care, education, and social programs. Many reparations activists favor the latter. Robinson proposes a trust fund for education, reparations from institutions that benefited from slavery, and continuing advocacy for civil

The New Freedmen's Bureau

Slave descendant Jack White is a writer for *Time* magazine who favors reparations for slavery. But instead of individual payouts, he believes that any funds paid as reparations should be put into social programs that would benefit African Americans. White explains:

> Use the money to uplift those who have been most hurt not only by the legacy of slavery but by existing discrimination and poverty: the urban and rural black poor. Put the money into a fund—call it the New Freedmen's Bureau—to finance the construction of schools, housing, transportation grids, factories, you name it, in the most depressed areas where the descendants of slaves are a majority. Use it to help finance new black-owned companies, to put poor black kids through college and endow cash-poor historically black universities, to run drug-treatment and job-training centers.

White estimates the United States owes slave descendants $24 trillion. He says that this money, if used in the way he has described, would fight "present-day injustice and social ills instead of futilely trying to atone for the sins of the past" by making individual payments to descendants of slaves, which he says would be "too much like hitting the lottery."

Jack E. White, "Sorry Isn't Good Enough," *Time*, June 30, 1997. www.time.com/time/magazine/article/0,9171,986599,00.html.

rights. Brooks proposes a museum of slavery as well. Others have suggested funding for job programs and housing, incentives to banks to give business loans to African Americans, scholarships, and educating all Americans about the history of African Americans. Asante sees the first step toward reparations as an official apology for slavery. He says, "To apologize is noble; not to apologize, in the light of the horrors of enslavement, segregation, and continuing discrimination, is arrogant."[79]

Asante further states that, while the cost of reparations for slavery will be huge, reparations do not need to be in the form of individual monetary payouts:

> Although it will cost billions of dollars, it will not have to be the doling out of billions of dollars of cash to individuals. While the delivery of money for other than cash distributions is different from most other reparations agreements, it is possible for reparations to be advanced in the United States by a number of other means. Among the potential options are educational, health care, land or property grants, and a combination of such grants. Any reparation remedy should deal with long-term issues in the African American community rather than a one-time cash payout.[80]

Another question is what exactly reparations for slavery would be for. As van Dyke asks, "Because those who were actual slaves are now dead, do their heirs have a continuing right to compensation? Is that right to compensation based on the wrong done to the ancestors, or to the continuing effects of that wrong that burden the descendants today, or both?"[81] The answers to these questions have a direct bearing on how much should be paid, in what form, and to whom. Unfortunately, there are no clear-cut answers to most of these questions.

Chapter Five

Are Reparations Necessary?

Much debate surrounds the issue of reparations for American slavery. Not everybody thinks that making payments to African Americans, either as individuals or as a group in the form of increased funding for social programs, is necessary or even a good idea. Some people argue that reparations would lead to resentment on the part of whites and further the second-class status of blacks. Others claim that Africans—as well as the nations of Africa—actually benefited from the institution of slavery, and therefore claims for reparations are redundant. And legal experts question the constitutionality of seeking reparations from the U.S. government. Opponents of these criticisms strongly defend the necessity of compensating African Americans for centuries of unpaid wages and denied opportunities. The fact that the reparations question is so controversial means it is not an issue that is likely to be resolved soon, if ever.

Did African Americans Benefit from Slavery?

One vocal opponent of reparations is author David Horowitz. In 2001 Horowitz placed an anti-reparations ad in the form of an essay titled "Ten Reasons Why Reparations for Slavery Is a Bad Idea —and Racist Too" in college newspapers across the United States. In the ad Horowitz argued, among other things, that blacks benefited from slavery by being brought from Africa to the more prosperous United States. He states: "The claim for reparations is premised on the false assumption that only whites have benefited from slavery. If slave labor created wealth for Americans, then obviously it has created wealth for black Americans as well, including the descendants of slaves."[82] Horowitz adds: "America's African-American citizens are the richest and most privileged black people alive—a bounty that is a direct result of the heritage [of slavery and its abolition] that is under assault."[83]

David Horowitz's anti-reparations essay appeared in this advertisement in the *Brown Daily Herald*.

Ten Reasons David Horowitz Opposes Reparations for Slavery

■

In 2001 David Horowitz placed an ad in college newspapers across the United States titled "Ten Reasons Why Reparations for Slavery Is a Bad Idea—and Racist Too." The following list outlines Horowitz's anti-reparations argument:

1. There Is No Single Group Clearly Responsible for the Crime of Slavery.

2. There Is No Single Group That Benefited Exclusively from Slavery.

3. Only a Minority of White Americans Owned Slaves, While Others Gave Their Lives to Free Them.

4. Most Living Americans Have No Connection (Direct or Indirect) to Slavery.

5. The Historical Precedents Used to Justify the Reparations Claim Do Not Apply, and the Claim Itself Is Based on Race Not Injury.

6. The Reparations Argument Is Based on the Unsubstantiated Claim That All African-Americans Suffer from the Economic Consequences of Slavery and Discrimination.

7. The Reparations Claim Is One More Attempt to Turn African-Americans into Victims. It Sends a Damaging Message to the African-American Community and to Others.

8. Reparations to African-Americans Have Already Been Paid.

9. What About the Debt Blacks Owe to America?

10. The Reparations Claim Is a Separatist Idea That Sets African-Americans Against the Nation That Gave Them Freedom.

David Horowitz, *Uncivil Wars: The Controversy over Reparations for Slavery.* San Francisco: Encounter, 2002, pp. 12–15.

The ad ignited a huge controversy. The fact that Horowitz is a white conservative makes his statements about African Americans sound racist to some people, but he is hardly alone in his views, nor is he the first to suggest that blacks benefited from slavery. Ward Connerly and Dinesh D'Souza, both black conservatives, have publicly agreed with Horowitz. So has black conservative Thomas Sowell, who asks, "Does anyone seriously suggest that blacks in America today would be better off if they were in Africa?"[84] Even the well-respected African American leader Booker T. Washington, who was born into slavery, wrote in his 1901 autobiography, *Up from Slavery:*

> The ten million Negroes inhabiting this country, who themselves or whose ancestors went through the school of American slavery, are in a stronger and more hopeful condition, materially, intellectually, morally, and religiously, than is true of an equal number of black people in any other portion of the globe. . . .

> Ever since I have been old enough to think for myself, I have entertained the idea that, notwithstanding the cruel wrongs inflicted upon us, the black man got nearly as much out of slavery as the white man did.[85]

Paying for Crimes They Did Not Commit

Many people believe that requiring Americans today to contribute to the bill for slave reparations is unfair. Steve Dasbach, the executive director of the Libertarian Party, says: "No one alive today had anything to do with the morally repugnant policy of slavery. So confiscating their money for reparations amounts to punishing people for crimes committed by someone else—more than 100 years ago."[86] Philosopher and author Janna Thompson explains this point of view further:

> The dead cannot be restored to life, their suffering cannot be assuaged, or their possessions restored to them. Past people cannot be made to pay for the injustices they committed, and no one living should be punished for the deeds of the dead. . . . Requiring that presently existing people make reparation for injustices done by their predecessors

seems to many people to be not all that different from punishing people for crimes they did not commit.[87]

U.S. president Bill Clinton was opposed to paying reparations
for slavery for a similar reason. According to an article from CNN,
Clinton was not in favor of "compensating the victims of slavery,
because the nation is so many generations removed from that era
that reparations for black Americans may not be possible."[88] But

---

President Clinton Opposed to Reparations

■

President Bill Clinton feared that apologizing and paying reparations for slavery could lead to further division between blacks
and whites. He was concerned not only about upsetting race relations but also about the possibility that an official apology
could be seen as an admission of guilt and open the door to legal action against the U.S. government. This excerpt describes
Clinton's visit to Africa in 1998, in which he discussed how
wrong slavery was but did not offer an apology for it.

> In stopovers in Africa [in March 1998], President Clin-
> ton was careful not to issue a formal apology for
> America's slave past, but rather to express regret and
> contrition. One reason . . . was to avoid being unnec-
> essarily divisive at home. But another important factor
> —rarely discussed by the White House—is concern
> over the legal implications of a formal apology. If Clin-
> ton, as head of the U.S. government, issues such a
> statement, it could increase legal, as well as moral,
> pressure for reparations to the descendants of slaves,
> much as many Japanese-Americans won reparations
> for their illegal incarceration at the outbreak of World
> War II. That could not only prove very expensive, it
> could itself further inflame racial tension.

U.S. News & World Report, "Jesse Jackson to the Rescue: White House Lauds His Support of Clinton on the Slavery Issue," March 29, 1998. www.usnews.com/usnews/politics/whispers/arti
cles/980406/archive_003640.htm.

Many poor blacks live in government-subsidized housing projects, including this one in New Orleans, Louisiana.

Robinson argues that reparations for slavery are still justified today. He describes slavery as "a human rights crime without parallel in the modern world" and says "it produces its victims *ad infinitum* [without end], long after the active stage of the crime has ended."[89]

Many people agree that blacks are entitled to reparations for the suffering of their ancestors, because this suffering and denial of equal opportunity continues to have a negative effect on the lives of blacks today. They point out that blacks have not had the same chances as whites to gain education and accrue wealth and other benefits that could then be passed on to their children. And Thompson argues that members of a nation do have historical obligations and a duty to repair past wrongs. She says, "The fact that our predecessors or forebears were the ones who did the wrongs does not excuse us from a responsibility for reparation."[90] This view is commonly held throughout the world, as van Dyke explains:

> The world has long recognized the enslavement of one person by another as one of the grossest violations of the fundamental human rights of individuals. The international community has also reached a solid consensus that all violations of human rights must be investigated and documented, that the perpetrators of

human rights abuses must be punished, and that the victims of human rights violations have a right to compensation. The obligation to investigate, punish, and provide compensation continues forward in time.[91]

Civil rights activist Malcolm X explained his views on why paying reparations today for something done by one's ancestors is the right thing to do: "If you are the son of a man who had a wealthy estate and you inherit your father's estate, you have to pay off the debts that your father incurred before he died. . . . Your father isn't here to pay. My father isn't here to collect. But I'm here to collect and you're here to pay."[92]

Could Reparations Increase Racial Hostility?

Some groups and individuals believe that paying reparations for slavery could increase racism. Speaking as a Libertarian, a political party that stresses individual liberties and minimal government interference in people's lives, Dasbach says, "Forcing people who had nothing to do with slavery to pay others who were never enslaved is the height of injustice and will only exacerbate racial tension in America." He adds, "Millions of white Americans who have no reason to dislike blacks may find one the moment they're forced to pay a race tax."[93] Another critic points to the anger that many people in Germany felt over the enormous war reparations their country was forced to pay after World War I and says, "Reparations can be dangerous. . . . Reparations breed envy and distrust and stir up hatred."[94]

Bittker agrees that reparations would increase racism, but for a different reason. In his book *The Case for Black Reparations*, he explains that any reparations payments that are based on race will, by necessity, require official definitions and classifications of race in order to determine eligibility. Bittker says:

I venture to predict that the adoption of a formal code of racial classification . . . would have calamitous consequences for the United States. It would ease the way to more and more private, public, and official distinctions between black and white. It would put pressure on millions of persons of mixed blood to make an official declaration of their racial origin.[95]

Some opponents of reparations argue that reparations would increase racism by implying that African Americans need extra

A French soldier stands on a shipment of coal sent by Germany as reparations. Germans were angry at being forced to pay reparations to France after World War I.

help in order to compete with whites. This same argument has been directed at affirmative action. One fourteen-year-old African American girl from Birmingham, Alabama, explains: "I actually think affirmative action adds to the racism problem today. I don't want white people to start thinking that blacks can't get anywhere in this world without special treatment."[96] Supreme Court justice Clarence Thomas, who attended Yale Law School in the early

1970s through the university's affirmative action program, explained that affirmative action made him feel like he had to work harder than fellow students. He says, "You had to prove yourself every day because the presumption was that you were dumb and didn't deserve to be there on merit."[97]

Author John McWhorter describes the racial harm he believes reparations to slave descendants would create in this country:

> There would be damage on both sides of the racial divide. As the magic transformations of the package inevitably failed to appear, the flop would be attributed to there not having been enough money granted. Next a new mantra would become established in the black community to cover the bitter disappointment: "They think they can treat us like animals for four hundred years and then just pay us off?" Meanwhile, non-blacks would begin to grouse "They got reparations—what are they still complaining about?" Whether these mutterings would be valid is beside the point, what matters is that they would arise and be passed on to a new generation, to further poison inter-racial relations in this country.[98]

Would Reparations Make Blacks into Victims?

Other critics argue that reparations would not only imply blacks need extra help, but would also reinforce the role of blacks being victims. Horowitz says, "To focus the social passions of African-Americans on what some Americans may have done to their ancestors fifty or a hundred and fifty years ago is to burden them with a crippling sense of victimhood."[99] Connerly agrees, saying, "We don't want young black kids to grow up thinking they are weak and can't look after themselves."[100]

Nationally syndicated columnist and talk show host Armstrong Williams believes the reparations movement encourages the view of blacks as inferior and is damaging to blacks. He says:

> As an American black, I find this stereotype of failure not only to be personally insulting, but also to be radically destabilizing. Simply to regard all members of a group as victims neatly removes such terms as "character" and "personal responsibility" from the cultural dialogue. After all,

what need is there for individual striving when it is plainly understood that all the difficulties that blacks suffer are the direct indisputable result of incidents that occurred centuries ago. The real danger of reparations, then, is that it presumes that being black is synonymous with being inferior. By extension, all blacks are encouraged to identify themselves as victims, even those who are plainly among society's privileged.[101]

No Amount Will Ever Be Enough

Some people say no amount of money can ever be enough to compensate African Americans for the horrors of slavery and its lingering aftereffects. Van Dyke says, "The final figure should indeed be very large, to give everyone involved a sense of honest closure, but . . . it will never be large enough to provide a true level of compensation for the losses that were suffered by so many generations of African Americans."[102] Still other people believe that any offer of money would be an insult to African Americans. Richard Lichtman, a law professor, wrote:

> The Negro's past suffering seems beyond the remedy of society to redeem. There is no payment that can supply its balance. It would be a sign of contempt for the Negro should the white community offer to compensate this debt, for there are trials of the spirit too large and awesome to stand comparison with any good that might be proposed as their measure. . . . The strictly compensatory act of payment for past suffering is impossible.[103]

Have Reparations Already Been Paid?

Other opponents of the reparations movement claim that African Americans have already been compensated for slavery—with the Civil War. Among those who say that the debt for slavery was paid with the lives of those who fought to end the practice are former Speaker of the House Newt Gingrich, columnist George F. Will, and conservative writer and editor Terence P. Jeffrey, who stated, "This nation did expiation for slavery in the form of a bloody Civil War that took the lives of almost 500,000 Americans, North and South."[104]

Critics of this argument point to the fact that the Civil War was not fought expressly to end slavery but rather to save the Union, and to the fact that even after slavery was abolished blacks in America continued to exist in a state of near-bondage for another century. As Brooks explains, "Ending slavery only to impose another, albeit less severe, system of racial subordination on blacks is more akin to a slap in the face than an apology or reparations for slavery."[105]

The reforms of the 1960s, including Johnson's Great Society, civil rights legislation, and the policy of affirmative action, are often cited as further examples of ways in which restitution for slavery has already been paid. Horowitz writes:

> Since the passage of the Civil Rights Acts and the advent of the Great Society in 1965, trillions of dollars in transfer payments have been made to African-Americans in the form of welfare benefits and racial preferences (in contracts, job placements and educational admissions)—all under the rationale of redressing historic racial grievances. It is said that reparations are necessary to achieve a healing between African-Americans and other Americans. If trillion-dollar restitutions and a wholesale rewriting of American law (in order to accommodate racial preferences) is not enough to achieve a "healing," what is?[106]

Reparations activists counter that because civil rights laws and affirmative action apply to women and other minorities, and not only blacks, these reforms cannot substitute for true reparations for slavery. In addition, African Americans have not received an official apology or an admission of responsibility for slavery and its legacy of racial segregation and discrimination.

The Historical Legality of Slavery

One argument against paying reparations to African Americans is that slavery was a universally acceptable practice at the time it occurred in the United States. Other nations around the world and throughout history practiced slavery, as far back as ancient Mesopotamia. Therefore, some people argue that it would not be fair to condemn the U.S. government for something that was not seen as wrong at the time.

Confederate and Union forces clash in Virginia in 1862. Some say the bloody Civil War that led to the end of slavery was payment enough.

However, as Brooks points out, by the time of the American Revolution most of the Western world no longer approved of slavery or viewed it a moral practice. Furthermore, Brooks says, "The American colonists were certainly aware of the changing global perspective on slavery, but they chose to ignore it." With the notable exception of Benjamin Franklin, virtually all of the founding fathers and writers of the Declaration of Independence and Constitution were slaveholders, as were eight of the first twelve U.S. presidents. These facts, Brooks argues, provide a rational basis for the government to compensate African Americans for the effects of slavery: "Clearly, then, American slavery was different. It kept alive a moribund institution—one that Western societies had marked for extinction due to its moral bankruptcy."[107]

Opponents of reparations argue in turn that since slavery was legal at the time it was practiced in the United States, there is technically no ground to seek restitution for slavery from the U.S. government. Slavery was not officially declared illegal until the ratification of the Thirteenth Amendment in 1865. In other words, technically speaking, no crime was committed by anyone holding human beings in bondage in the nation before 1865.

Forgiving and Forgetting

In an article titled "Reparations Now," conservative columnist and editor of *National Review Online* Jonah Goldberg says that reparations are an apology and as such, should mean the end of racial problems in the United States. Goldberg explains:

> The whole point of reparations is that they provide closure. Reparations are, in effect, an apology. And if you take the money then you are accepting the apology. If you accept an apology then you must also forgive. And forgiving means forgetting.

> And what a wonderful thing forgetting would be. I could be in favor of reparations if it spelled the end of things, not the beginning. No more racial guilt-mongering, no more racial blackmail. The long national nightmare would be over. Programs designed to make up for the past would also be a thing of the past. Affirmative action, quotas, set-asides, all of it would go. We could finally get back to being the forward-looking country we're supposed to be.

Jonah Goldberg, "Reparations Now," *National Review Online*, March 19, 2001. www.national review.com/goldberg/goldbergprint031901.html.

African American residents of Washington, D.C., celebrate the passage of the Thirteenth Amendment, which declared slavery illegal.

And the U.S. Constitution forbids what are known as ex post facto laws—retroactive laws that criminalize actions that were legal at the time they occurred.

In addition, the legal principle of sovereign immunity makes it very difficult to seek reparations from the government at all. *Sovereign immunity* means that nations, or sovereigns, are exempt from lawsuits by private citizens. In the United States, as in other countries, the federal government cannot be sued without its permission. However, reparations activists point out that the government can, and often does, waive sovereign immunity and consent to being sued. In fact, some say that the right to claim sovereign immunity has already been waived, since slavery and in particular the transatlantic slave trade are seen as crimes against humanity, which are not entitled to the protections of sovereign immunity.

The Future of Slave Reparations

The question of whether slave reparations will ever become a reality in the United States remains open. Many people see it as unlikely. Bittker says that he sees "no likelihood that today's courts would hold that a right to compensation had been inherited by the descendants of the emancipated slaves."[108] Williams explains why he believes reparations legislation is not likely to be passed: "If it literally paid to be a victim, countless people would rush forward to adopt the mantle. Plainly, forcing this government to pay reparations to the biological, cultural, or religious offshoots of every group that they wronged over the past two hundred years would bankrupt this country. For this reason, reparations have no chance of becoming a reality."[109]

Farmer-Paellmann believes that the doctrine of sovereign immunity will prove to be insurmountable, because she says it is "unlikely that the federal government would ever give African Americans permission to sue it for slavery reparations."[110] She points to the fact that Conyers's proposal to study the continuing effects of slavery on today's African Americans, H.R. 40, has yet to make it out of committee. But Conyers has vowed to continue to reintroduce the bill in Congress each year until it is passed into law. He says:

> At the end of the day, we will look upon all of the struggles of Africans in America leading up to this final effort of achieving redress for the crimes committed against them and their ancestors. It will be a movement that will unite Africans in America with Africans from around the globe and show humanity that crimes against Africans in the form of enslavement and colonialism is an issue of justice that must be made right.[111]

It seems likely that more lawsuits such as those brought by Farmer-Paellmann, N'COBRA, and the NAACP will be brought against corporations. Additional formal apologies like those from Virginia and Maryland may be on the way from other states, and more states may follow the example of California, making business declare their past ties to slavery. If enough states pass such laws, perhaps they will become national policy. In any case, the issue of reparations for slavery is far from being resolved, and so it is likely to continue to be debated for a long time.

Yet Adjoa A. Aiyetoro, a founding member of N'COBRA, is optimistic about the future of slavery reparations: "We are convinced more than ever that victory is on the horizon and will be ushered into manifestation by strong organizational work, unity, and the wings of the ancestors."[112]

Notes

Introduction: The Legacy of Slavery

1. Quoted in American Renaissance, "Halle Berry: Hollywood Is Racist," January 28, 2005. www.amren. com/mtnews/archives/2005/01/halle_berry_hol.php.

2. Quoted in Internet Movie Database, "Biography for Halle Berry." http://imdb.com/name/nm0000932/bio.

3. Molefi Kete Asante, *Erasing Racism: The Survival of the American Nation*. Amherst, NY: Prometheus, 2003, p. 246.

4. Quoted in Ronald P. Salzberger and Mary C. Turck, eds., *Reparations for Slavery: A Reader*. Lanham, MD: Rowman & Littlefield, 2004, p.134.

5. John David Smith, *Black Voices from Reconstruction, 1865–1877*. Gainesville: University Press of Florida, 1997, p. 152.

6. Quoted in Bob Gibson, "Slavery Apology Measure Ignites Legislative Debate," *Daily Progress*, January 16, 2007. www.dailyprogress.com/servlet/Satellite?pagename=CDP/MGArticle/CDP_BasicArticle&c=MGArticle&cid=114919 2673260.

7. Raymond A. Winbush, ed., *Should America Pay? Slavery and the Raging Debate on Reparations*. New York: HarperCollins, 2003, p. 59.

8. Quoted in Roy L. Brooks, *Atonement and Forgiveness: A New Model for Black Reparations*. Berkeley: University of California Press, 2004, p. 207.

9. Brooks, *Atonement and Forgiveness*, p. 8.

Chapter One: What Are Reparations for Slavery?

10. National Coalition of Blacks for Reparations in America (N'COBRA), "What Is Reparations?" www.ncobra.org/aboutus.htm.

11. Winbush, *Should America Pay?* p. xxii.

12. Brooks, *Atonement and Forgiveness*, p. 20.

13. Brooks, *Atonement and Forgiveness*, pp. 187–88.

14. Quoted in Brooks, *Atonement and Forgiveness*, p. 185.

15. Asante, *Erasing Racism*, p. 263.

16. Quoted in Smith, *Black Voices from Reconstruction*, p. 62.

17. Quoted in Randall Robinson, *The Debt: What America Owes to Blacks*. New York: Dutton, 2000, p. 226.

18. Len Cooper, "Slavery Did Not End with the Civil War," Len Cooper's Village, June 16, 1996. www.great linx.com/peonage.htm.

19. Lisa Delpit, *Other People's Children: Cultural Conflict in the Classroom.* New York: New Press, 1995, p. 92.

20. Asante, *Erasing Racism*, p. 186.

21. Asante, *Erasing Racism*, p. 8.

22. Robinson, *The Debt*, p. 8.

23. Brooks, *Atonement and Forgiveness*, p. ix.

Chapter Two: Early Efforts at Reparations

24. Quoted in Roy L. Brooks, ed., *When Sorry Isn't Enough: The Controversy over Apologies and Reparations for Human Injustice.* New York: New York University Press, 1999, p. 365.

25. Quoted in Brooks, *Atonement and Forgiveness*, p. 120.

26. Quoted in Winbush, *Should America Pay?* p. 15.

27. Mary Frances Berry, *My Face Is Black Is True: Callie House and the Struggle for Ex-Slave Reparations.* New York: Knopf, 2005, p. 12.

28. Berry, *My Face Is Black Is True*, p. 11.

29. Salzberger and Turck, *Reparations for Slavery*, p. 67.

30. Gerene L. Freeman, "What About My 40 Acres and a Mule?" Yale-New Haven Teachers Institute. www.yale.edu/ynhti/curriculum/units/1994/4/94.04.01.x.html#b.

31. Quoted in Berry, *My Face Is Black Is True*, p. 73.

32. Quoted in Berry, *My Face Is Black Is True*, p. 50.

33. Quoted in Berry, *My Face Is Black Is True*, p. 39.

34. Quoted in Berry, *My Face Is Black Is True*, p. 180.

35. Berry, *My Face Is Black Is True*, p. 182.

36. Quoted in Winbush, *Should America Pay?* p. 27.

37. Quoted in Berry, *My Face Is Black Is True*, p. 223.

38. Quoted in Berry, *My Face Is Black Is True*, p. 224.

Chapter Three: Reparations Today

39. Robert Mann, *The Walls of Jericho: Lyndon Johnson, Hubert Humphrey, Richard Russell, and the Struggle for Civil Rights.* San Diego: Harcourt Brace, 1996, p. 376.

40. Quoted in Marcus Epstein, "Myths of Martin Luther King," Lew Rockwell.com, January 18, 2003. www.lewrockwell.com/orig/epstein9.html.

41. Quoted in Millions for Reparations, "In the News," www.millionsforreparations.com.

42. Quoted in Mann, *The Walls of Jericho*, p. 503.

43. Quoted in Lyndon Baines Johnson Library and Museum, "President Lyndon B. Johnson's Commencement Address at Howard University: 'To Fulfill These Rights.'" www.lbjlib.utexas.edu/johnson/archives.hom/speeches.hom/650604.asp.

44. Quoted in Boris I. Bittker, *The Case for Black Reparations*. Boston: Beacon, 2003, p. 161.

45. Quoted in Bittker, *The Case for Black Reparations*, p. 167.

46. Quoted in Bittker, *The Case for Black Reparations*, p. 168.

47. Quoted in Bittker, *The Case for Black Reparations*, p. 27.

48. Quoted in Salzberger and Turck, *Reparations for Slavery*, p. 75.

49. Quoted in Mary Frances Berry and John W. Blassingame, *Long Memory: The Black Experience in America*. New York: Oxford Univeristy Press, 1982, p. 406.

50. John Conyers Jr., "Major Issues— Reparations," Congressman John Conyers, Jr. www.house.gov/ conyers/news_reparations.htm.

51. Quoted in Salzberger and Turck, *Reparations for Slavery*, p. 91.

52. Quoted in Congressman Tony P. Hall, "Hall Calls on Congress to Apologize for Slavery," June 19, 2000. www.directblackaction. com/tony_hall.htm.

53. Quoted in Peter Viles, "Suit Seeks Billions in Slave Reparations," *CNN*, March 27, 2002. http:// archives.cnn.com/2002/LAW/03/2 6/slavery.reparations.

54. Deadria Farmer-Paellmann, "Personal Testimony of Deadria Farmer-Paellmann in Support of H. R. 40—Commission to Study Reparations Proposals for African Americans Act," National Coalition of Blacks for Reparations in America (N'COBRA). www. ncobra.org/pdffiles/DEADRIA%20 april%206%20statement.pdf.

55. Quoted in Brian DeBose, "NAACP to Target Businesses," *Washington Times*, July 12, 2005. www. washtimes.com/national/2005071 2-120944-7745r.htm.

56. Quoted in Payton Hoegh, "Jackson Welcomes Slavery Apology but Sees 'Obligation to Repair Damage Done,'" CNSNews.com, February 2, 2007. www.cnsnews.com/View Nation.asp?Page=/Nation/archive/ 200702/NAT20070202a.html.

57. Quoted in Larry O'Dell, "Virginia Lawmakers Pass Slavery Apology," Associated Press, February 24, 2007. http://news.aol.com/ topnews/articles/_a/virginia- lawmakers-pass-slavery- apology/2007022421140999000 2?ncid=NWS00010000000001.

58. Quoted in Jeninne Lee-St. John, "Should States Apologize for Slavery?" *Time*, March 27, 2007. www.time.com/time/nation/article /0,8599,1603581,00.html.

Chapter Four: The Complexities of Reparations

59. Quoted in Winbush, *Should America Pay?* p. 103.

60. Quoted in Winbush, *Should America Pay?* p. 73.

61. Quoted in Winbush, *Should America Pay?* p. 76.

62. Quoted in Winbush, *Should America Pay?* p. 58.

63. Quoted in Janna Thompson, *Taking Responsibility for the Past: Reparation and Historical Injustice.* Cambridge, UK: Polity, 2002, p. xvii.

64. Quoted in Gibson, "Slavery Apology Measure Ignites Legislative Debate."

65. Salzberger and Turck, *Reparations for Slavery*, p. xii.

66. Quoted in Winbush, *Should America Pay?* pp. 72–73.

67. Brooks, *Atonement and Forgiveness*, p. 190.

68. Quoted in Winbush, *Should America Pay?* p. 75.

69. Asante, *Erasing Racism*, p. 19.

70. Salzberger and Turck, *Reparations for Slavery*, p. xii.

71. Quoted in Salzberger and Turck, *Reparations for Slavery*, p. 143.

72. Quoted in Winbush, *Should America Pay?* p. 73.

73. Brooks, *Atonement and Forgiveness*, p. 190.

74. Quoted in Salzberger and Turck, *Reparations for Slavery*, p. 148.

75. Bittker, *The Case for Black Reparations*, p. 95.

76. Quoted in Salzberger and Turck, *Reparations for Slavery*, p. 148.

77. Jonah Goldberg, "Reparations Now," *National Review Online*, March 19, 2001. www.national review.com/goldberg/goldbergprint 031901.html.

78. N'COBRA, "How Much Is Owed?" www.ncobra.com/ncobra_info.htm.

79. Asante, *Erasing Racism*, p. 236.

80. Asante, *Erasing Racism*, p. 264.

81. Quoted in Winbush, *Should America Pay?* p. 58.

Chapter Five: Are Reparations Necessary?

82. David Horowitz, *Uncivil Wars: The Controversy over Reparations for Slavery.* San Francisco: Encounter, 2002, p. 12.

83. Horowitz, *Uncivil Wars*, pp. 15–16.

84. Quoted in Horowitz, *Uncivil Wars*, p. 130.

85. Quoted in Bartleby.com, "Booker T. Washington: Up from Slavery: I. A Slave Among Slaves." www. bartleby.com/1004/1.html.

86. Quoted in Chuckhawks.com, "Libertarian Party Press Release: Slavery Reparations." www. chuckhawks.com/lprelease_slavery _reparations.htm.

87. Thompson, *Taking Responsibility for the Past*, p. xii.

88. CNN.com, "Clinton Opposes Slavery Reparations," June 17, 1997. www.cnn.com/ALL POLITICS/1997/06/17/clinton.race.

89. Robinson, *The Debt*, p. 216.

90. Thompson, *Taking Responsibility for the Past*, p. xviii.

91. Quoted in Winbush, *Should America Pay?* p. 57.

92. Quoted in Millions for Reparations, "In the News."

93. Quoted in Chuckhawks.com, "Libertarian Party Press Release: Slavery Reparations."

94. Quoted in Salzberger and Turck, *Reparations for Slavery*, p. 99.

95. Bittker, *The Case for Black Reparations*, p. 97.
96. Quoted in Laurel Holliday, *Dreaming in Color, Living in Black and White: Our Own Stories of Growing Up Black in America*. New York: Archway, 2000, p. 165.
97. Quoted in Martin H. Simon, "Supreme Mystery," *Newsweek*, September 9, 1991, p. 28.
98. John McWhorter, "Blood Money," *American Enterprise*, July/August 2001. www.taemag.com/issues/articleid.15514/article_detail.asp.
99. Quoted in Salzberger and Turck, *Reparations for Slavery*, p. 129.
100. Quoted in Brooks, *Atonement and Forgiveness*, p. 41.
101. Quoted in Winbush, *Should America Pay?* p. 167.
102. Quoted in Winbush, *Should America Pay?* p. 74.
103. Quoted in Salzberger and Turck, *Reparations for Slavery*, p. 90.
104. Quoted in Terence P. Jeffrey, "Clinton Apologizes to Africa for Sins the U.S. Never Committed," FindArticles, April 3, 1998. http://calbears.findarticles.com/p/articles/mi_qa3827/is_199804/ai_n8788125.
105. Brooks, *Atonement and Forgiveness*, p. 194.
106. Horowitz, *Uncivil Wars*, p. 14.
107. Brooks, *Atonement and Forgiveness*, p. 187.
108. Bittker, *The Case for Black Reparations*, pp. 3–4.
109. Quoted in Winbush, *Should America Pay?* p. 170.
110. Quoted in Winbush, *Should America Pay?* p. 25.
111. Quoted in Winbush, *Should America Pay?* pp. 20–21.
112. Quoted in Winbush, *Should America Pay?* p. 225.

Chronology

1619
Twenty African indentured servants land at Jamestown, Virginia, becoming the first Africans in the British colonies.

1788
The U.S. Constitution is ratified; Article I states that slaves count as three-fifths of a person in determining taxation and representation.

1830s
Laws are passed in the United States that forbid anyone to teach blacks to read or write and punish blacks for preaching from the Bible.

1857
The Supreme Court rules in the *Dred Scott* case that blacks are not citizens and have no rights.

1863
President Abraham Lincoln signs the Emancipation Proclamation, freeing slaves in the Confederate states.

1865
The Civil War ends; the Thirteenth Amendment is passed, abolishing slavery. William T. Sherman issues Special Field Order No. 15, which is quickly reversed by President Andrew Johnson.

1866
The Southern Homestead Act grants freed slaves land in southern states at a low cost; only about a thousand freedmen receive homesteads.

1868
The Fourteenth Amendment is ratified, granting full U.S. citizenship to African Americans.

1870
The Fifteenth Amendment is ratified, granting black males the right to vote.

1875
The Civil Rights Act of 1875 bars segregation in public places.

1883
The Civil Rights Act of 1875 is declared unconstitutional by the U.S. Supreme Court.

1896
The U.S. Supreme Court rules in *Plessy v. Ferguson* that separate but equal facilities for blacks and whites are constitutional.

1899
Former slave Callie House founds the National Ex-Slave Mutual Relief, Bounty, and Pension Association.

1909
The National Association for the Advancement of Colored People (NAACP) is founded in New York City.

1954

In *Brown v. Board of Education*, the U.S. Supreme Court reverses its earlier decision in *Plessy v. Ferguson* and bans segregated schools.

1964

The Civil Rights Act of 1964 is passed, creating the Equal Employment Opportunity Commission and prohibiting discrimination in hiring. Martin Luther King Jr. receives the Nobel Peace Prize.

1965

Malcolm X is assassinated in New York City. The Voting Rights Act bans literacy tests before voting.

1971

The U.S. Supreme Court issues a ruling that allows busing for school desegregation.

1989

Representative John Conyers of Michigan introduces a proposal for a commission to study reparations for slavery and continues to introduce the same proposal every year.

1996

California votes to ban affirmative action in government employment and college admissions. Similar bans are soon passed in Washington and Florida.

2000

Representative Tony Hall introduces H.R. 356, a proposal to acknowledge and apologize for slavery.

2007

Virginia becomes the first U.S. state to issue a public apology for its role in slavery.

For More Information

Books

William Kweku Asare, *Slavery Reparations in Perspective*. Victoria, BC: Trafford, 2002. In this book the author discusses the necessity of dealing with the issues of the transatlantic slave trade, slavery, and reparations.

Mary Frances Berry, *My Face Is Black Is True: Callie House and the Struggle for Ex-Slave Reparations*. New York: Knopf, 2005. This book traces the efforts of Callie House to obtain pensions for former slaves in the early part of the twentieth century.

Alfred L. Brophy, *Reparations Pro and Con*. New York: Oxford University Press, 2006. This book covers both sides of the debate over reparations for slavery.

James Haley, ed., *Reparations for American Slavery*. San Diego: Greenhaven, 2004. This book offers nine essays from leading figures on both sides of the reparations debate.

John Torpey, *Making Whole What Has Been Smashed: On Reparations Politics*. Cambridge, MA: Harvard University Press, 2006. In this book John Torpey explains the politics of the global reparations movement.

Internet Sources

African American Registry, "Queen Mother Witnessed Much History." www.aaregistry.com/african_american_history/1022.

Associated Press, "Advocates Quietly Push for Slavery Reparations," MSNBC, July 9, 2006. www.msnbc.msncom/id/13785355.

Claudia Cowan, "California Considering Slave Reparations," Fox News.com, May 6, 2002. www.foxnews.com/story/0%2C2933%2C52062%2C00.html.

FoxNews.com, "Second Slave Reparations Suit Filed," May 2, 2002. www.foxnews.com/story/0%2C2933%2C51723%2C00.html.

John McWhorter, "Blood Money," *American Enterprise*. www.taemag.com/issues/articleid.15514/article_detail.asp.

NPR, "Making Amends: Debate Continues over Reparations for U.S. Slavery," August 27, 2001. www.npr.org/programs/specials/racism/010827.reparations.html.

Web Sites

The Afrocentric Experience (www.swagga.com/index.shtml). This Web site provides numerous links to information pertaining to African Americans, including the slave reparations movement.

Afrocentric.Info (www.afrocentric.info). This Web site provides numerous links to topics of concern to African Americans, including information on reparations for slavery.

CURE—Caucasians United for Reparations and Emancipation (www.reparationsthecure.org/index.shtml). This organization of white Americans is dedicated to seeking reparations for African Americans for slavery.

Millions for Reparations (www.millionsforreparations.com). This Web site provides links to articles and information about activities concerning the reparations movement.

N'COBRA (The National Coalition of Blacks for Reparations in America) (www.ncobra.org). Founded in 1987, this group works to obtain reparations for African American slave descendants.

Reparations Central (www.reparationscentral.com/index.html). This Web site serves as a clearinghouse of information on the issue of reparations for slavery. Contains links to other organizations as well.

Slavery Reparations Information Center, Project 21 (www.project21.org/Reparations.html). This page of the Project 21 Web site offers links to numerous articles on the slavery reparations issue.

Index

Picture Credits

Cover photo: AP Images
AP Images, 7, 11, 25, 43, 45, 47, 57, 75
© Bettmann/Corbis, 52
The Bridgeman Art Library/Getty Images, 21
© DePALMA/Classic Stock/The Image Works, 35
© Najlah Feanny/Corbis SABA, 49
Hulton Archive/Getty Images, 41, 58, 85
© Ed Kashi/Corbis, 9
The Library of Congress, 19, 22, 31, 38, 66
Mary Evans Picture Library/The Image Works, 29
MPI/Getty Images, 87
National Archives and Records Administration, 14
© North Wind Picture Archives, 64, 69
© Private Collection/Peter Newark American Pictures/The Bridgeman
    Art Library, 17, 33
John Anthony Rizzo/UpperCut Images/Getty Images, 61
Chip Somodevilla/Getty Images, 55
Mario Tama/Getty Images, 79
Three Lions/Hulton Archive/Getty Images, 81
Time & Life Pictures/Getty Images, 18

About the Author

Cherese Cartlidge holds a bachelor's degree in psychology and a master's degree in middle school education. She has taught reading, language arts, and math. Cartlidge currently works as a freelance writer and editor. This is her sixth book for Lucent Books.